MEDICO-TOPOGRAPHICAL REPORT

ON

ZANZIBAR.

BY

JOHN ROBB, M.D.,

SURGEON, BOMBAY MEDICAL ESTABLISHMENT.

CALCUTTA:
OFFICE OF THE SUPERINTENDENT OF GOVERNMENT PRINTING.
1879.

CALCUTTA :

PRINTED BY THE SUPERINTENDENT OF GOVERNMENT PRINTING,
8, HASTINGS STREET.

FROM

    JOHN KIRK, Esq.,
        Her Majesty's Agent and Consul-General, Zanzibar,

To

    The SECRETARY to the GOVERNMENT of INDIA,
               FOREIGN DEPARTMENT, CALCUTTA.

Zanzibar, 5th March 1879.

SIR,

       I have the honour to forward herewith a valuable report on the climate of Zanzibar, prepared from observations carefully taken by Dr. Robb, Agency Surgeon here.

    2. I would venture to suggest that, as this is the first complete record ever made of the climate of this place, it might be thought expedient to have the tables published for reference.

    3. I would call attention to Dr. Robb's forwarding letter, in which he requests that this report may be forwarded to the Medical Department. I would also mention that information on the climate of Zanzibar has been asked for by Mr. Carrington, the Registrar of Wrecks, Marine Survey Department, Calcutta, and that I have stated in reply that this report was about to be forwarded.

              I have the honour to be,
                   SIR,
            Your most obedient Servant,

                JOHN KIRK,
       Her Majesty's Agent and Consul-General, Zanzibar.

FROM

    Surgeon JOHN ROBB, M.D.,
        Civil Surgeon, Zanzibar,

To

    The POLITICAL AGENT,
        ZANZIBAR.

Zanzibar, 4th March 1879.

Sir,

    I have the honour to request that you will forward to the Government of India the accompanying Medico-Topographical Report on Zanzibar, to which are attached the results of the meteorological observations of five years.

    This report is submitted in fulfilment of the further condition required for my promotion, and I have to beg that you will intimate this fact to the Supreme Government for the information of the authorities at Bombay.

        I have the honour to be,
           Sir,
          Your most obedient Servant,

         JOHN ROBB, M.D., *Surgeon,*
           Civil Surgeon, Zanzibar.

CONTENTS.

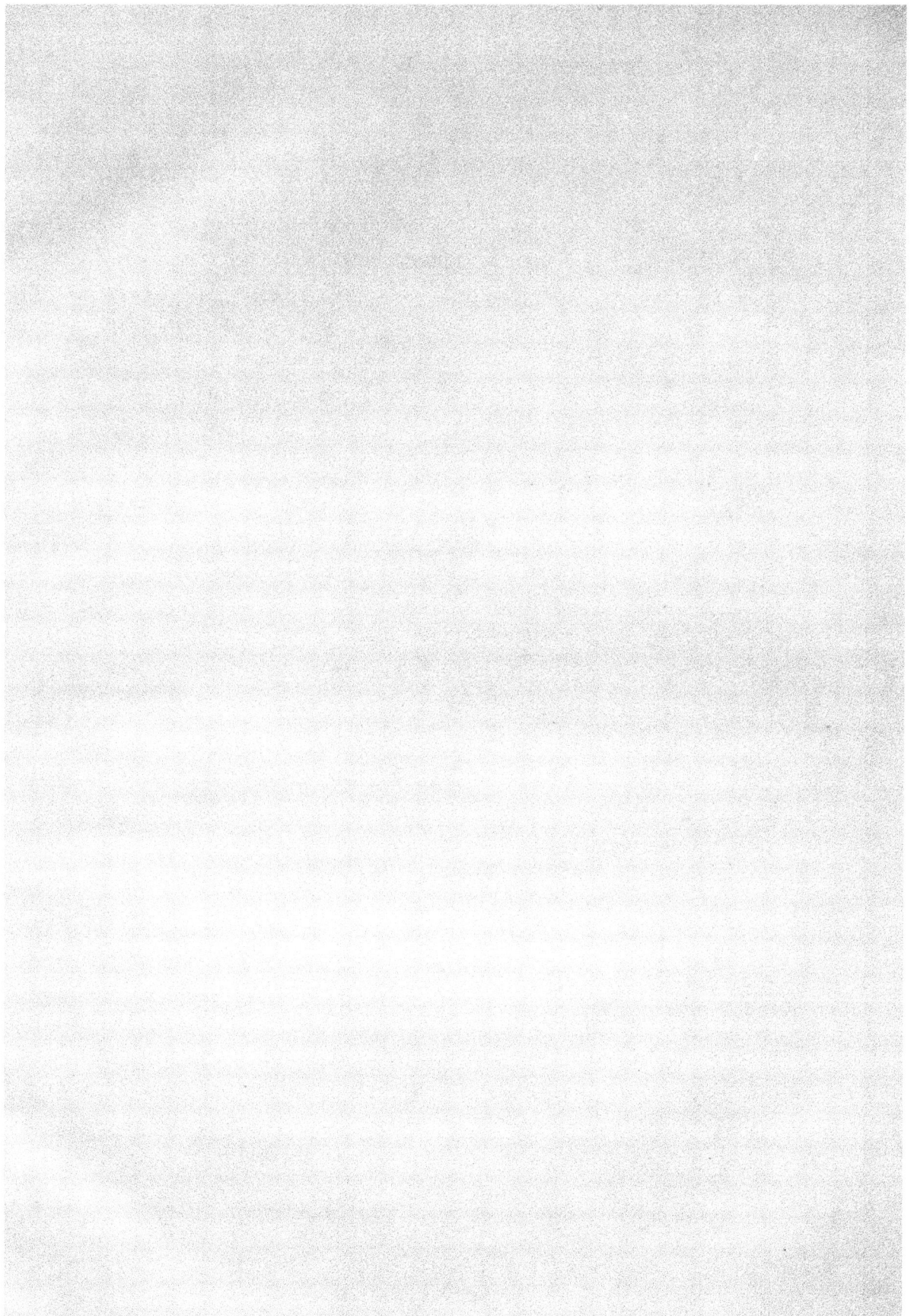

38° E.   38° 30′

Pangani River

Pemba Islands

Pangani

Nasseon Point

5° 30′   5° 30′

Zanzibar
Channel

Kipumbwe River

Kipumbwe

Map of
ZANZIBAR ISLAND,
AND
ADJACENT COAST of AFRICA.

From the Admiralty Charts
reduced.

Ras Nungwe

African
Mainland

Tumbatu
Island

200 ft

Ras Oreweombe

Kokotoni

6.6   6° 6′

Z a n z i b a r

Saadani

I s l a n d

Ras Wena

Chucho Head

Bawy Ish   Harbour   170
10   Dunga
80 ft   Zanzibar   C. Imaka

Ras Wiridi

Wami River

Ras Buyu
Chumbi Is.

Winde

Ras Nahanduchi
40 ft

Bagamoyo

Z a n z i b a r
C h a n n e l

Ras Kizimkazi

6° 30′   6° 30′

Kingani River

600 ft

1000 ft

Ras Kunkadya

M a i n l a n d

of A f r i c a

Daree Salam

[Sd.]   JOHN ROBB, M.D., Surgeon.

Zanzibar, E. Africa, 18th Jany. 1879.

Ras Kimbiji

7°   7°

38° E.   38° 30′

LITHOGRAPHED FROM AN ORIGINAL SUPPLIED BY THE FOREIGN DEPARTMENT.
at the Surveyor General's Office, Calcutta, May 1879.

35° 14′ 20″ E.

Changa Isd

Nehandoho Isd

Tumba   Chapani Isd

Ras el Ras □

Mto Mlandedi

Mto Rozzi

Mtoni Village

Chim chim spring

Mtoni

Msangini 440 feet

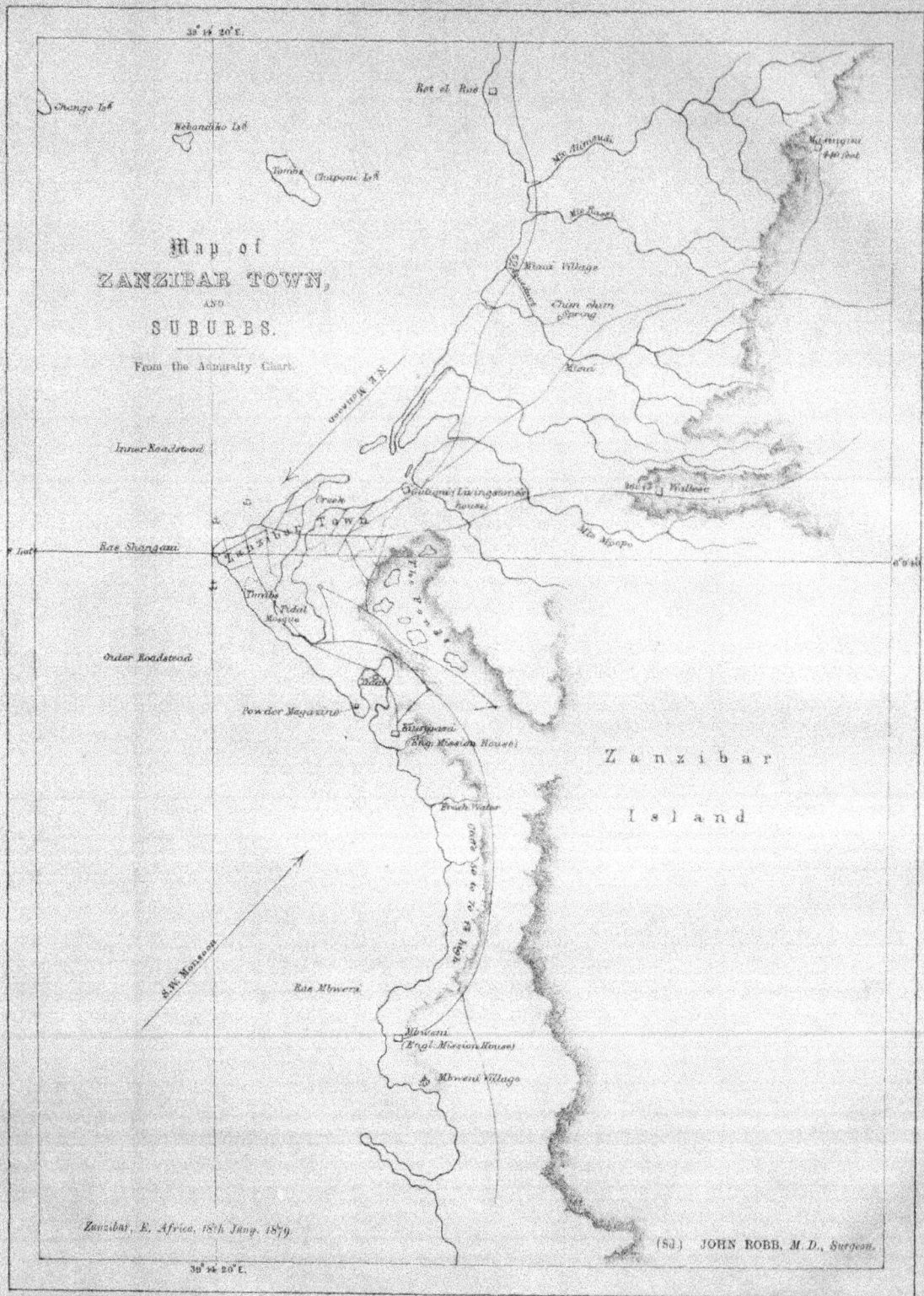

Map of
ZANZIBAR TOWN,
AND
SUBURBS.

From the Admiralty Chart.

N.E. Monsoon

Inner Roadstead

Creek

Dudoni (Livingstones) house

Mto Mjopo

Mill Welbeck

TOWN

ZANZIBAR

6° 0′ 0″

7° Inlt   Ras Shangani

Throbs

Tidal Mosque

Beach

Outer Roadstead

Powder Magazine

Shanganni (Engl. Mission House)

Fresh Water

S.W. Monsoon

Z a n z i b a r

I s l a n d

Ras Mbweni

Mbweni (Engl. Mission Houses)

Mbweni Village

Zanzibar, E. Africa, 18th Jany. 1879.

(Sd.)   JOHN ROBB, M. D., Surgeon.

35° 14′ 20″ E.

LITHOGRAPHED FROM AN ORIGINAL SUPPLIED BY THE FOREIGN DEPARTMENT,
at the Surveyor General's Office, Calcutta, May 1879.

MEDICO-TOPOGRAPHICAL REPORT

ON

ZANZIBAR.

BESIDES the Island of Zanzibar and the neighbouring Pemba Islands, the territorial coast possessions of His Highness Seyed Burghash are said to extend from about three degrees north of the River Jub, bordering Somaliland, in the north, as far south as Cape Delgado, which is a headland near the middle of the east coast of Africa, and marks the northern limit of the Portuguese possessions. The name and influence of His Highness extend as far west as Lake Tanganyika, and, although his claim to authority over the various tribes of the interior in that direction is but a nominal one, his patronage and support are of importance, and are, as a rule, freely granted to travellers and others proceeding into the interior. The section of the continent of Africa thus roughly defined has a seaboard of nearly 800 miles, is estimated to cover an area of about 20,000 square miles, and supports a population reckoned to number half a million.

Burton says the continental islands of Africa " have proved equally useful as
The Island.
forts impregnable to the wild aborigines and as depôts for exports and imports. Second to none in importance is Zanzibar, and the future promises it a still higher destiny." The promise of the future is in process of execution, and during the past five years of personal acquaintance with the place, there have been many improvements which are material and of importance. Insignificant in size as Zanzibar Island looks on the map, alongside the great bulk of Africa, it has nevertheless no mean place in the history of commerce. It is not in itself a wealthy island, and its value as a possession is derived chiefly from its close connection with the fertile and productive mainland and with the rich clove-yielding Island of Pemba, a short distance to the north and east. Its chief town, called also Zanzibar, possesses a commodious and sheltered natural harbour, open towards, and within sight of, the mainland opposite. This town is the seat of the local Government, and where the American, British, French, and German Consuls have their residences. The American and German are known as trading Consuls,—that is, they are merchants vested with consular powers. The British and French Agencies are strictly diplomatic.

The island is situated about midway between Aden and Natal, at a distance
Geography.
of about 1,700 miles from each of these places, and is about 2,400 miles in a direct line from Bombay. It lies in a direction from N.N.W. to S.S.E., between south latitudes 5° 43′ and 6° 28′ 35″, and between east longitudes 39° 8′ 30″ and 39° 14′. It thus stretches through little more than three-quarters of a degree, its extreme length being about 52½ English miles from Ras Nungwé, the north point, to Ras Kizimkazi, the farthest point south. The breadth of the island varies considerably, owing to its irregular and broken coast line; but its greatest uninterrupted breadth is 27 English miles in a direct line east from the English Mission House at Mbweni, a few miles south of the town. From this same point

A

due west to the coast of the mainland at Ras Windi, the distance is also 27 English miles, and this is the average breadth of the waterway between the island and the mainland, which varies from 25 to 30 miles. The island has never, I believe, been surveyed, but it is said to cover an area of about 400,000 acres. It is more than twice the size of Malta, and rather less than half the size of Cyprus,—our newest dependency,—also in the Mediterranean.

Zanzibar Island is described by Dr. Christie ("Cholera Epidemics in East Africa") as of coralline formation, "erected on a base of stratified sandstone...... The madrepore structure is evidently based upon the summits of an abrupt and sharp-rising submarine range, which, of course, must have been under the ocean-level at some remote period. By the action of the gradually subsiding waters, a coralline conglomerate has been formed. On the southern and eastern parts of the island the deposit is more scanty, merely filling up the interstices of the coral rag, leaving exposed the bare summits, and making travelling, except by foot, exceedingly difficult. Where sufficient deposits have been left, the soil is fertile and the crops early, the porous understructure carrying off superfluous rains, but still retaining moisture and heat." The greatest elevation of the surface of the island is 440 feet above sea-level, according to recent measurements, and this height is reached a short distance north-east of the town on the hilly ridge that traverses the island interruptedly in its long axis, only a few miles distant from its west coast. The crop-yielding section of the island is that occupying chiefly the western tract, which, in gently undulating slopes, reaches away from this central ridge to the sea-level. This is the leeward aspect, and it is in this direction that all madrepore islands are said to grow, while it is well protected from the long-continued force of the south-west monsoon. A few short streams intersect this fertile tract and discharge themselves into the sea, forming at their mouths with the reflux of the tide dense mangrove swamps where the land is low and level. It is in localities such as these, found chiefly at the mouths of the larger rivers of the mainland opposite, that are bred "the agues, dysenteries, diarrhœas, deadly fevers, and other ills to which flesh is heir." The eastern slope of the island is in some parts fertile and populous, though generally towards its southern limits it is a waste and barren district, for a great portion of the year exposed to the desolating influence of the south-west monsoon. From all accounts of the natives, this is, however, the healthy division of the island. And it would seem that in earlier times health was before wealth, for the ancient capital of the island was on the eastern coast, "and the place is still called Unguja Mku, Old Unguja." At the present day, the native name of the town of Zanzibar is Unguja.

Near the middle of the west shore of the island is Ras Shangāni, a triangular spit of land, on which is built the town of Zanzibar. It is fixed in 6° 9′ 40″ south latitude, and 39° 14′ 20″ east longitude. There is an old and a new town, and they are divided from each other naturally by a tidal creek, which, opening from the foreshore looking north, runs up along the back of the older and main portion of the town. At the spring tide of 20th March 1878, the highest in the memory of "the oldest inhabitant," the water in the creek reached so far as to leave only a narrow sandy ridge, less than 200 yards across on the southern side of the spit, to connect the old town with the body of the island. This ridge cut across deeply would insulate the town at the time of high tides. The newest portion of the town has for some years been gradually extending into the country beyond the creek, over which, at its narrowest part, there is a bridge of solid masonry in two divisions.

The Town.

This inlet spreads over a large area of soil which is entirely covered at high tides, and at these times a broad sheet of water contributes a picturesque feature to the landscape. It is when the tide ebbs and the whiting is washed from the sepulchre that there is left exposed to the influence of a burning tropical sun a large expanse of black soft mud, impregnated with the sewage refuse of a populous neighbourhood. There are at first sight all the conditions necessary to make this locality specially obnoxious and the hotbed of bowel complaints and of fevers of a typho-malarial type. Yet, regarding the crowded neighbourhood literally fringing the old town

The Creek.

Formation.

side of the creek and including the town residence, church, and other buildings of the Universities' Mission, the medical history of five years points to little of an exceptional nature that can be justly attributed to soil exhalations. Whatever the accurate scientific explanation may be, no doubt much in favour of the creek is due to the fact of its being tidal and covered over twice a day for several hours at a time with brackish water; and its general course also is such that the winds of the north-east and south-west monsoons sweep up and down rather than across it during the greater portion of the year. Its ventilation is thorough. It would only be in shutting out the tide and by disturbing the soil in the course of possible changes that any immediate exceptional unhealthiness of the locality would be likely to arise. At all times, an objectionable feature is when the dead bodies of bullocks, camels, donkeys, &c., consigned to the creek are floated up by the tide and left to putrefy, and to contaminate with the most offensive odours the only "airing" ground within easy reach of the town. A nuisance of this kind is the rule and not the exception; and a stranger strolling over this "lung" of Zanzibar—surely a diseased one—remarks on the number of bones scattered about in all states of petrifaction, some already bleached white, and others just picked clean by the packs of pariah dogs that scour the plain at night. A roadway is in process of formation across the upper border of the creek, and when it is completed, the slight detour into the country rendered necessary at high tides will be avoided.

The spit of land on which the town is situated divides a safe and commodious harbour into a north and south anchorage. A chain

Harbour.

of islets, coral reefs, and sandbanks protects the harbour by forming an effective natural breakwater to the swell and currents of the main channel. The islets are a common formation in these latitudes, and are built up by the gradual and constant deposit of sand and coral *débris* on the submarine reefs by the action of the sea. They are covered with a thin surface of black vegetable mould—the products of decomposition. These islets, together with the Island of Zanzibar itself, may be viewed as an example of the atoll, a type prevailing near the equator, and the harbour is the encircled lagoon. The area of the harbour between these outlying islets and the main island is given at about 4 square miles. It varies in depth from 7 to 14 fathoms, but the usual anchorages are taken up in 9 or 10 fathoms and within easy access of the shore by boats at all times of the tide. With each change of the tide, which has an average rise of $12\frac{1}{2}$ feet, there is a strong sea current flowing alternately out and in. Spring tides rise 15 feet and neaps 10 feet. The front or inner north harbour which the town looks out upon is occupied by a native and foreign shipping during the long-continued southerly winds; while the outer anchorage or back bay is taken advantage of during the two or three months—December to February—when the north-east monsoon blows its freshest. The inner anchorage is the more important one, not only because it is available during the greater portion of the year, but also, and chiefly, because time and labour are economised in the working of cargoes. The central Custom House, and most of the European and American merchant houses, are ranged along this aspect. Low tides especially occasion much difficulty and inconvenience in the loading and unloading of cargo boats. The boats must lie off in water sufficiently deep to float them when loaded, and it is almost a daily occurrence to witness files of labourers of both sexes passing with their loads to and from the boats, often waist deep in filthy mud and water. It is believed that local prejudice and superstition are ranged against staking off a portion of the foreshore to facilitate shipping interests; for the same reason probably that on a certain occasion stirred up opposition to the planting of a foreign flagstaff in the soil. Such measures are viewed with disfavour, as meaning or foreboding appropriation. But superstition must yield to necessity, and it is evident that a pier or jetty to facilitate the working of cargoes must soon find a place in the programme of projected improvements. Hitherto, the ornamental chiefly has outrun the practically useful. The navigable waterway for "making" the harbour from the north and from the south is carefully buoyed off, but only during the day-time is it considered safe to enter the port. Occasionally, a good moon and the knowledge that comes from long experience have made it possible to get up to the harbour anchorage after sunset; but the practice, being attended with a certain amount

B

of risk, is discouraged. It would be no great difficulty to fix leading lights; but who is to pay? And besides very few of the residents would care to be introduced to correspondence and business during the hours set apart for sleep.

In Zanzibar there is hardly a single street worthy of the name, as we think of it. The town is a curious and haphazard jumble of misleading lanes and provoking *culs-de-sac*. To a stranger they are extremely bewildering, especially when he gets away from the landing places into the heart of the town. It would be well nigh impossible to lay down a street chart; but the necessity for such a thing has not yet come. There are only two "lions" in the place, and they have not yet passed into history; they are *bonâ fide* living ones, and are to be found without any difficulty confined in a den near the Sultan's Palace. The principal thoroughfare runs east and west past the Palace, but, except in this neighbourhood, it is like most of the others, narrow and tortuous. From this main street as a base, lanes branch away through the town, breaking off at all conceivable angles, and in continually changing direction and breadth. The recent introduction of wheeled conveyances called for the demolition of houses, the rounding off of awkward corners, and there followed the sweeping away of doorsteps and any of the usual Arab lounges or barazas that interfered with the gauge required for safe transit into the country. On the whole, however, there is marked improvement since Bishop Steere wrote that "no picture of a street in Zanzibar would be complete without two or three cows or a bull of a small breed with humps looking for something green."

Streets.

The houses are in keeping with the streets. They are of all sorts and sizes in the same quarter, and they have evidently been built anyhow and anywhere, without regard to order or straight lines. Gradually, new ideas, sprinkled with a little taste, are being imported, and progress is already marked by the improvements that adorn the Sultan's Palace both outside and inside. The higher and well-to-do classes of the community live in substantial stone-built houses, but the teeming slave population who do not live in the houses of their masters, and the labouring classes generally, occupy huts of wattle and dab, roofed over with grass or plaited palm leaves, while some are contented with a more unpretending structure still, "composed of a rude framework of poles, surrounded by old matting, and covered with a sloping roof of palm leaves." Except the German Consulate, which was built on a European plan from the foundation, nearly all the residences of the Americans and Europeans are Arab-built houses originally, adapted by alterations and additions to the requirements of Western civilisation. They are almost all located in the west end of the town, and so closely huddled together that it would be no great difficulty for a resident to visit his neighbours by passing from one house to another without going down into the street at all. Like all oriental houses, the roofs are flat and "chunamed," and serve as airing grounds in the cool afternoons, and for sleeping on by those who are rash enough to risk the results of "a cool night outside." It is common to see on the roofs of the native houses mats and ordinary kitandas (charpoys) lying about; for here in dry weather some of the inmates are compelled to pass the night in order to relieve the pressure upon the confined and already crowded sleeping space within. To the merchant these flat roofs serve another important purpose. Cloves and "peppers" (chillies), cowries and copal, hides and coir rope, are each in their turn and season spread out on the roofs in the sun to be dried and cleaned; and it is unnecessary to explain that cowries and hides and "peppers" when thus out for an airing make themselves known from afar. An Arab house has often been described. The large block of building forming the present British Consulate is a good specimen of one, though many of its original features have of course been lost in its present occupation. There is the usual central court, and round this are built the various reception and sleeping rooms. These rooms do not, as a rule, communicate with each other, but are self-contained and entered from the common corridor that runs round the court in front of them. The house may be two or three storeys high, the ground floor being devoted to store and lumber rooms, with perhaps a reception hall having a stone bench or seat built round about it; while on the higher floors would be the cook-room, bath-rooms, public and private sitting-rooms, and bed-rooms. The

Buildings.

furnishings are extremely simple, often comfortless and tawdry even in high quarters. But where refinement and luxury are affected in the exhibition of a miscellaneous assortment of mirrors, carpets, wonderful pictures, and yet more wonderful old china, there is grotesquely evident an utter ignorance of the fitness of things for tasteful display. The houses of the British-Indian subjects vary among themselves in size and convenience according to the social position of the owner or tenant. All are more or less filthy, and, with the exception of about half a dozen, they do not in any way represent the wealth of the occupant. These houses do not have the inner court, which is a useful ventilator, but are a collection of rooms and holes and corners on a ground floor and upper floor, the connection between which is usually a ricketty and uncertain trap-ladder, alongside of which dangles a greasy forbidding rope by way of hand-rail. The front rooms on the ground floor are, as a rule, set apart as shops for retail business, or as offices where the establishment is larger and engaged in whole-sale transactions. In many cases these shops and offices are during the night-time converted into bed-rooms. The rooms or courts at the back of the houses —sometimes upstairs, sometimes below—are used as cook-rooms, bath-rooms, or general store-rooms, and it has often been noticed that the bath-room and the cook-room have not the most sanitary relation to each other. Between the shop in front and the places at the back of the house there are usually other rooms or closets, which have not credit enough to enable them to borrow a little light from their neighbouring apartments. It is in such places the sick of the house-hold are stowed away, and a patient has to be groped for in Egyptian darkness, which a sickly oil *buttie* struggles unwillingly to dispel. The smaller these Moslem houses are—and it is chiefly those occupied by the Khojahs and Borahs that have been described—the more thickly do they seem to swarm with inmates of all sexes and ages, among whom are domestics drawn from the slave popu-lation. How such households pass the night may be more easily imagined than described. With the Banyan merchants and others of the Hindoo caste, the case is different: their houses are, as a rule, larger and less crowded; for only members of their own caste can serve them, and they have not yet seen their way clear to introduce their wives and children from India. The Goanese community follow more closely the European mode of life, but with them, too, in most cases, it is rather a rush and a struggle to be rich than to live comfort-ably and in health. Their persons are tidier and smarter than their houses. The few public buildings include the mosques, the Custom House, and the Fort. A large English church, a clock tower, and a *hummâm* or public baths, are progressing rapidly towards completion. The mosques, according to Burton, are "useful, but by no means ornamental, 'meeting-houses' scattered about the city for the use of the 'established church.' They are oblong rooms, with stuccoed walls and matted floors: the flat roofs are supported by dwarf rows of square piers and polygonal columns; whilst Saracenic arches, broad, pointed, and lanceolated, and windows low placed for convenience of expectoration, with inner emarginations in the normal shape of scallops or crescents, divide the interior." Tombs are to be met with anywhere in the town as well as in the country, and sometimes they turn up in an unlooked-for corner. The Custom House, the Fort, and the clock tower are all quite close to the Palace. The Custom House has lately been improved in appearance, but at the sacrifice of a portion of its enclosed space required to widen the thoroughfare outside it. It was never before sufficiently large for the business it has to control; and although a covered shed has been erected within the Custom House boundaries nearer the beach, the place is still hampered and much wanting in warehouse accom-modation. The customs, hitherto farmed by the Banyans, are now in the hands of the Khojahs; and since August of 1876 the well-known Tharia Topun has been Customs Master. The Fort is a clumsy imposing pile of masonry, and at many points dilapidated. Burton describes it as "one of those naïve crenelated structures flanked by polygonal towers, each pierced for one small gun, and connected by the comparatively low curtains in which our ancestors put their trust. A narrow open space runs round it, and it is faced by a straight-lined detached battery," placed on the beach, and roofed over with corrugated zinc sheeting. The Fort, as it is, must be looked upon as utterly useless for defensive purposes. Its walls enclose a large collection of huts in grand confusion. They are the abodes of the soldiers and other dependants connected with the Fort.

The clock tower is rising up on the beach opposite the Palace; and in the town, on the site of the old slave market, the church referred to, founded on Christmas Day, 1873, is now having the roof thrown over it. This work, when completed, will be a lasting monument to patience and perseverance in the face of manifold difficulties, and to the possibilities of native labour under wise superintendence. The Barracks ought to be noticed in passing. A recently organised regiment, numbering in all about 600 youths and boys, required some kind of accommodation, not so much for "quarters" as for a drill and parade ground. A suitable place was found, and is now in good working order. The "men" live as yet spread over the town as was their wont in civil life. It is astonishing to what a pitch of efficiency in drill these lads have been brought by an enthusiastic and hard-working English naval officer. Among improvements, an important feature is the harbour embankment or sea-wall. It has already advanced from the Custom House Bunder past the Sultan's Palace, Harem, and workshops, and in front of several large Arab and European houses as far as the Salt Fish Market in the Malindi quarter. It is said that His Highness wishes to carry this embankment and marine parade round the foreshore, so that he may be able to drive out into the country without having to pass through the difficult and somewhat dangerous thoroughfares. This embankment is lit up at night with kerosine lamps placed at regular intervals, and a visitor who remembers the place half a dozen years ago would be struck with the grand appearance presented to the harbour. The main street is also lit up at night for a short distance from the Palace on both sides of it. Beyond these points is impenetrable gloom, and a resident going out at night has to be piloted along by the help of his own private lantern. Outside the town and along the shore to the north are several detached Arab houses, passed in coming into harbour; while south of the town are the Powder Magazine on the beach, and farther distant, on a higher level, two separate residences of the Universities' Mission. The Government buildings have all good positions. They consist of the New Consulate, a house known as the Jail Building near it, the Old Consulate occupied by the Assistant Political Agent, in a low room of which is the Post Office, and the house known as the Surgeon's quarters. The New Consulate has been considerably altered and added to since it was purchased from the Universities' Mission in 1874. The court and the offices are on the ground floor looking out upon the sea, and the property as a whole seems in every way well adapted for an official residence. It has, however, its full share, with the other houses along the foreshore, of the highly offensive smell given out from the beach at low tides and in certain directions of the wind. It may be that, owing to the action of the tides and currents under the influence of the prevailing wind, there is at this point a greater harbour sewage silt than to be met with elsewhere; and so large is the quantity of sulphuretted hydrogen given out from the low-tide beach, that white-painted boats left on the beach for even half an hour have had their bottoms quite blackened.

There are a few so-called hotels in the town, but they are all very mediocre, some of an inferior description.

Schools are mostly in name only, and have no local habitation. Here and there all over the town, in any place that is convenient,

Schools.

some of the native children are to be met with, gathered together chiefly to chant the Koran and the usual prayers; and to repeat these, probably without understanding their meaning, is to be finished as regards a liberal education. The text-book is the Koran itself, and where the Arabic characters and figures are taught, the "slate" used is a polished scapula of the camel or ox. In one or two places Guzerati is taught to the Indian children that can be got together. A high standard is not required for the purposes of trade, and to be able to read and to write and to do a little arithmetic is proficiency. A Parsee, in an endeavour to improve matters in this direction, has recently opened Guzerati and English classes at a low fixed charge for the Indian children principally, but as yet he has met with small encouragement. The parents are, as a rule, lamentably wanting in education themselves, but they are perhaps prosperous traders and therefore satisfied. They grudge to pay even a nominal charge for the education of their children; and among the Khojahs, who form the great majority of the Indian Mahommedans in

Zanzibar, it is said that schools are viewed with suspicion, particularly where strange text-books are introduced and English is taught, for they fear lest the rising generation should grow up to dispute the position and spiritual importance ascribed to their High Priest, Agha Khan.

The population of the island is estimated at 150,000, and that of the town variously from 60,000 to 100,000. The larger number is probably not in excess of the town population during the months of the north-east monsoon, December to March. During these months there is a considerable influx of north country tribes from Oman, Hadramaut, and Sheher in Arabia, from the Island of Socotra, and from the ports of the Somali and Galla countries. The population at this time is said to be increased by one-fifth or even more. There are also numerous fresh arrivals from Bombay and Cutch, but these are mostly reliefs for those about to depart by the return dhows in the south-west monsoon. It is evident that the population is at all times a very mixed one, made up of Arabs of various tribes and half-castes; of Waswahili or the coloured free people; of numerous slaves drawn from various tribes of the interior and mostly domesticated; of natives of Comoro, Johanna, and Madagascar; of a number of Persians and so-called Abyssinians, these last being generally connected with the Sultan's establishments. Besides these, there are Parsees, Hindus, Moslems, and Goanese from India; and last of all are the few Europeans and Americans. The original islanders are the Wahadimu and the Watumbatu: the former, now few in number, occupy the central and eastern parts of the island, and devote themselves chiefly to agriculture; while the Watumbatu, belonging to the Island of Tumbatu, near the north-west point of Zanzibar Island, are mostly a seafaring people, employed as fishermen or as sailors in the small craft engaged in local traffic. It is impossible to estimate the number of the Arab-protected population, and the following figures are only an approximation to the number of British-Indian subjects and of the white residents on shore at the present date:—

Races.	Men.	Women.	Children.	Total.	Remarks.
American	5	1	1	7	On the coast of the mainland and in the interior, with protection from Zanzibar, and including the French and English Mission stations at Bagamoyo and Monobasah, there are in all about 30 men, 7 women, 1 child.
British, including English Mission	21	9	10	40	
German and Swiss . . .	16	3	5	24	
French, including French Roman Catholic Mission .	12	8	...	20	
Total white residents .	...	...	...	91	
Goanese	229	8	9	246	Numbers of British-Indians are spread up and down the coast of the mainland, but amongst these the Bhattia caste of the Hindus is in greatest force; they are said to number about 800, in the Zanzibar dominions, exclusive of the small proportion remaining in the Town of Zanzibar.
Parsees	16	2	4	22	
Hindus, including—					
Bhattias	200	...	...	} 380	
Wanias	140	...	...		
Hajjams	30	1	2		
Sonars	7	...			
Mahomedans, including—					
Khojahs	1,300	700	Children included under Men and Women according to sex.	2,000	
Borahs	200	100		300	
Mehmons, including Khatris, Sonars, Sindhis, &c. .	125	5		200	
Total coloured residents .	...	...	...	3,148	
GRAND TOTAL . .	...	...	...	3,239	

There has been a steady, though unimportant, increase of Indian settlers of all castes from year to year; but owing, no doubt, in part to recent times of distress in India, the increase this year is greater than at any former period. No doubt, also, increased facilities of communication and extended knowledge of the place and its promises of lucrative trade have been the means of pushing forward emigration from Western India. All new comers do not find it easy readily to settle down in Zanzibar itself, and they are in time drawn off to the various ports of the mainland. As has been observed, the Bhattias chiefly establish themselves

c

on the mainland, where they find easier terms of living and better profits. The Moslems, on the other hand, stick to the town, probably because of their closer connection with the foreign import trade. All these classes of Indian subjects come mostly from Cutch, Surat, Bombay, Goa, and the native state of Jamnuggur; they are to be met with from Merka in the Somali country as far south as Mozambique and Delagoa Bay, and a few find profitable occupation at one or more of the Comoro Islands and at some of the Madagascar ports. There may be small independent traders among these, but, as a rule, they are the agents of mercantile houses in Zanzibar, or are directly connected with Bombay and Cutch.

There are no sanitary measures of any kind in force in Zanzibar to preserve and protect the health of the community; and that the place has during the past eight years escaped the visit of any formidable epidemic is matter for sober congratulation. This immunity has not been purchased, and it certainly has not been worked for. The appearance of an epidemic would occasion far more alarm than surprise, and any one fairly well acquainted with Zanzibar knows how ready the insanitary condition of the town is to give length and breadth to the spread of an epidemic, and it has been well said that a plague can do terrible mischief in the congenial sphere of an Oriental city, when it settles down to its work among the dirt and the inhabitants. One or two leading thoroughfares are swept and in order, and a passing visitor, whose duty or pleasure limits his wanderings to these, expresses himself satisfied that Zanzibar is greatly abused. It is not in such well-kept streets that epidemic disease lingers and grows; they are but as a clean front put on to cover filth and wretchedness lying thickly behind, and it is necessary to leave these and to go into the heart of the town and into the houses of its densely populated parts to be able to recognise the truth of Dr. Christie's remarks, that "so long as the inhabitants are content with the existing state of affairs, they must reap the consequences—disease and death. If excrementitious matter be not removed from dwelling-houses and the vicinity of wells, then the inhabitants must eat it, drink it, and inhale it, and this is by far the most expensive mode of getting quit of it." Accumulations of surface refuse are very often left to be scoured away by the rains, but the rains are not always heavy enough to ensure a thorough flushing, and perhaps the mass is too bulky to be moved forward, so that the surface drains become constantly choked and soon create nuisance both to eye and nose. This is more frequently the case with the underground drains, which, in a place like Zanzibar, ought not to exist at all. Everything of the kind should be carefully laid down, but always uncovered, so that the nucleus of a nuisance could be detected at once and removed. These superficial drains, whether covered or uncovered, have however nothing or very little to do with the disposal of bath-room and water-closet sewage, and this is the serious difficulty connected with Zanzibar sanitation. The ordinary *chironi* or privy is a built well or shaft sunk a short distance below the foundations of the house. The top of the shaft may be on the ground floor only, or it may be on the higher floors; and it is not uncommon to see a round, tapering, chimney-like arrangement passing away up from the ground to the apartment where the convenience is required. A large house may require two or three of these conveniences, but they have no connection with each other unless below ground, where sewage filtration and soakage go on as they have gone on for generations past, until the subsoil of Zanzibar has become little better than an enormous cesspool. It is unnecessary to explain how dangerous to health must be the character of the town wells, at least in such circumstances; for, though made use of constantly, they are otherwise utterly neglected, and it is impossible to see that they can escape being highly charged with organic impurities. It is to the use of waters such as these wells would supply, far more than to climate *per se*, that is to be traced the great amount of sickness and mortality met with chiefly amongst the Indian population. A well-planned system of sewers is said to be possible of construction without much difficulty and at no very great expense.

Sanitation.

"Zanzibar city and island is plentifully supplied with bad drinking water." This statement of Burton's has reference to twenty years ago, and it is equally true at the present time.

Water-supply.

During all these years no satisfactory progress has been made towards a healthier condition of the water-supply, and it is in this direction chiefly that a decrease of sickness and mortality is to be looked for. The coloured inhabitants are the principal consumers of this necessary of life, and they are also the chief sufferers from debilitating diseases, such as may in justice be attributed to the quality of the water in constant use. The white residents do not suffer in the same degree, because more care is taken with regard to the source from which their water for domestic purposes is derived. No doubt other reasons for their immunity from water-diseases would be given by many of the residents themselves, but to a fairly good description of water used by them must be given the first place. The sources of the present water-supply for domestic purposes are various. There are many wells scattered all over the town, and others in the neighbouring shambas or plantations, which are made use of by the natives; there is Mwara spring about 6 miles away towards the interior of the island; the better known Chim-Chim spring a few miles north of the town near the sea; and rain-water tanks of iron or of stone. The harbour ship *London* is self-supplied with condensed water, which is used for all purposes. In existing circumstances on shore, the most reliable source of supply is the rain-water tank, more or less inconstant of course, because depending upon the rainfall, which, under the tropics, has no equable distribution over the months of the year. To store rain-water in Zanzibar, it is necessary to have (1) an iron tank of good capacity, or a carefully-built masonry tank, under or above ground, completely protected from soil filtration by a uniform coating of the best cement, and from extraneous matters by a proper covering removable for cleansing purposes; (2) a collecting area, which is the flat roof common to most of the houses, European and native,—a surface well beaten down and "chunamed" over, having a watershed in one or more directions to carry away the rain as desired to (3) the conducting pipes, which are usually made of tin. With a large enough tank, almost every house of the Europeans and upper class natives has roof area sufficient to collect rain-water for its own uses. But the purposes which many of the roofs are made to serve lead to unavoidable waste. It would be evidently useless to collect rain-water from roofs devoted to the drying of copal, cowries, hides, &c., and the requirements of trade are always likely to submerge all higher-considerations. A private supply of rain-water being therefore in many cases out of the question, the next best source is the Chim-Chim spring at Mtoni. Here it is usual for vessels going to sea to take in their water-supply; but, without care, it is possible even at this important source to store a very impure water. The aqueduct at Mtoni leads from the pure spring into a large open tank, which has an exit pipe leading to the sea. The open tank is used by the natives for the washing of their bodies and clothes, and laziness or ignorance may be the cause of much danger by drawing water from this outlet pipe instead of from the aqueduct above the tank. Another spring at Boo-booboo, a mile or two further north, yields a water very similar in quality to that of the Mtoni spring. It divides with Mtoni the supply of the shipping, but it is too far away to be much used by the inhabitants. The Mwara spring already noticed is patronised chiefly by the Arabs, who are said to be very particular about their drinking-water, and who employ their slaves to bring it from the most approved source, no matter how distant that may be. On Burton's authority, "the purest element is found at Kokotoni, a settlement on the north-west coast of the island." But whatever kind of water is used, it ought always to be subjected to careful filtration, if not to previous boiling; and that it is impossible to be too watchful concerning the water for domestic use, will be at once granted on reading Dr. Christie's remarks on this point. His authority is the latest and the best, and I make no apology for the liberty I take in borrowing largely from his book (already mentioned) on a subject of vital importance. He writes: "The potable water of Zanzibar may be said, without any exaggeration, to consist of the diluted drainage of dunghills and graveyards—a saturated solution of every conceivable abomination...... It may be said, without fear of contradiction, that there is not a single well in the town of Zanzibar that is not contaminated, and that the most of them are so to the greatest possible degree..... I have no doubt whatever but that the water-supply of Zanzibar has much to do with the spread of disease, but more especially with the causation of several diseases common in the place," and "it will be admitted by all that water con-

taining the filtrations of graveyards and privies is unfit for human use, is loath-
some to all civilised beings, and can only be voluntarily used by a class of
people with tastes little higher than the brute creation. . . . . . The town wells are
all open at the top, and they are never cleaned out unless they become completely choked up. They are almost flush with the ground, and are merely
slightly elevated round the brink, so as to prevent the water of the streets from
flowing into them. Some are on the sides of the streets, and accidents occasionally occur from people falling into them." These extracts tell of a serious
state of matters, and further revelations shake confidence in the so-called Chim-
Chim water. No matter how trustworthy servants are supposed to be, the best
of them, it is to be feared, will readily enough connive at deception, so long as
they believe it possible for their misconduct to escape detection. "Europeans,
resident in the town, ... pay well for having a supply brought daily from this
place (Chim-Chim), but they seldom if ever get it. There is plenty of good
water to be got, but it is next to impossible to get it for any money, ... the
trouble being too great. The female water-carriers, although paid highly to
bring a small supply of good water from a distance, frequently bring it to
Europeans from the town wells, and, when allowed to do as they like, unchecked
for a time, bring it from the nearest town well, and, during the rains, they even
collect it from the thatch of their own huts. A common plan is for half of a
water party to go to the country to bring water which is sweet or fresh, while
the other half sit down at one of the half brackish town wells and await the
return of the others. They then mix the water, and, with the banana leaf tied
over the mouth of the jar, bring it to the house as pure spring-water. To get a
Negress to act otherwise is simply impossible, and only Arabs can manage to get
a purer element. . . . . . . There is nothing more calculated to excite one with
horror and disgust at the whole Negro race than the sight of the water-women at
the shamba (country) well-pits. These pits are simply excavations in the sandy
soil to about the depth of 10 feet or more, gradually narrowing towards the
bottom, and generally situated on a sloping ground. There is seldom, during
the dry season, more than a few inches of water at the bottom of these pits, and
round the top about thirty or forty women, with their water-jars, are squatted,
waiting for the percolation of the water. This, one after another, they ladle
into their water-jars by means of a cocoanut shell fastened to a long·stick, and
this work generally occupies two or three hours. Meanwhile, the gossip goes
on. The border of the pit is used as a convenience; and, as the women adopt
the custom of washing Moslem fashion, there are other ingredients mixed up
with the excreta, the frequenters of the well-pits belonging, for the most part,
to the Corinthian order of ladies." This is a fearful picture to contemplate, but
in no single particular are its graphic details overdrawn. The following analysis
of well waters is summarised from information given in Dr. Christie's work
(pages 289 to 297). The "samples were collected after the close of the heavy
rains in the month of May. This will account for a considerable amount of
vegetable impurities, and also for the absence of other impurities of a more
deleterious nature." The analysis seems to be a fair estimate of the potable
waters procurable at Zanzibar, and points to the urgency of the need for some
such organisation as that of a Water Police.

Analysis of Zanzibar Water.

No. 1.—*Well in yard of an American house, situated near the sea-
        beach—*

> Water used for washing copal, &c., not generally for drinking or
>   cooking.
> Thick black deposit of decomposing organic matter.
> Perfectly saturated with sulphuretted hydrogen, fumes of which
>   escaped on opening sample bottle.
> Lime, magnesia, chlorine, sulphuric acid, in large quantity; iron,
>   traces only.
> Brackish taste, therefore not taken to drink.
> Organic matter in large quantity.
> Prolonged boiling required to free this water from sulphuretted
>   hydrogen.

No. 2.—*Town wells near the beach*—
> Slight smell of sulphuretted hydrogen on opening bottle.
> Free carbonic acid in large quantity.
> Sulphates and chlorides of lime abundant.
> Deposit: organic vegetable matter, with numerous crystals of carbonate of lime.
> Remarks: this water most impure as regards inorganic ingredients; is hardly fit for drinking purposes.

No. 3.—*Town well*—
> Organic matter abundant.
> Moistened lead paper held in mouth of bottle, without touching the water, instantly blackened.
> On exposure to air becomes milky from escape of carbonic acid gas and deposit of lime.
> Boiling gives a deposit of shining films of phosphate of lime, traces of magnesia, and of sulphuric acid; large amount of chlorine, combined with lime and magnesia.
> Deposit: organic vegetable matter.
> Microscope reveals diatoms.
> Remarks: this is the best well in the town and that in general use.

No. 4.—*Mwara spring, in the interior of the island, 5 or 6 miles from the town*—
> Water perfectly sweet.
> Sulphuretted hydrogen, no smell.
> Free carbonic acid none.
> Lime abundant.
> Sulphuric acid none.
> Chlorine abundant.
> Deposit: fresh undecomposed vegetable matter.
> Microscope: diatoms numerous, among which an undetermined species of *Hyalodiscus*.
> Remarks: considered to be the finest water in the island, and is highly prized by the Arabs.

No. 5.—*Country wells or shamba water*—
> Sulphuretted hydrogen and a strong fæcal smell on opening bottle.
> Lime (chlorides and sulphates), small quantity.
> Iron, traces only.
> Organic matter in large amount in solution, and in black offensive deposit.
> Remarks: most highly prized drinking water among the Negroes of Zanzibar, because of its sweetness; but it is undoubtedly the water that produces the *lumbrici* that so frequently and severely afflict the juvenile population of the town. "Europeans will not touch it owing to its white colour, it being something like diluted skim milk." They forget at the same time that a "water may be clear and fresh to the taste, and still be exceedingly impure, containing organic matter and inorganic salts in solution in large quantity."

No. 6.—*Water from cement tanks*—
> Organic matter in small quantity.
> Sulphuretted hydrogen, slight trace.
> Lime, small amount; no sulphates; chlorides, slight deposit.
> Organic vegetable matter, small deposit.
> Remarks: this water is quite pure when compared with that from the wells.

No. 7.—*Mtoni water*—
> Clear; no sulphuretted hydrogen and no disagreeable smell.
> Free carbonic acid; considerable amount of lime; faint traces of sulphuric acid; large amount of chlorine.
> Carbonate of lime crystals on sides of bottle like fine sand.
> Deposit: fresh vegetable matter without sign of decomposition.
> Microscope: diatoms, among which numerous species of *Pleurosigma*.

D

No. 8.—*Booboobo water*—
>   Free carbonic acid.
>   Carbonate of lime crystals as in No. 7, like which specimen of water this one is almost identical.
>   Contained living specimens of the sun animalcule, active and healthy.

The streams which supplied the last two samples "are identical in quality at their source, but they are polluted to a different degree in their passage to the beach, the channel of the former being much clearer than that of the latter. . . . . . . The samples sent for analysis were taken from the streams in the evening, when it was in flood, and seem to have been then free from excrementitious impurities." To remedy a state of matters so disastrous to the health of the community, something more permanently effective than even a Water Police Force is required ; and certainly no great public work would more honourably mark out the rule of His Highness Seyed Burghash than the introduction of a constant supply of good drinking-water to his town. Mtoni is the nearest best supply, and the engineering difficulties attending a scheme of water-works from this point are said to be insignificant. This work would be a worthy diversion for a portion of the wealth that is flowing out in other directions, and it is believed that a beginning has already been made in the direction referred to. Evidently His Highness is earnestly enthusiastic in developing the capabilities of his capital and possessions generally. Fancy armies and gorgeous equipages cost much money, but they have no doubt their own special use and are not to be despised. The display of wealth and power is inseparable from the dignity belonging to all governing races of the earth, and it is peculiarly a component part of the Oriental idea of importance.

On a review of the character of the water-supply of Zanzibar, taken in connection with the filthy state of the town itself, *Quarantine.* and the unclean and utterly careless habits of the people, it is not to be wondered at that so much unfavourable to the place has been written and spoken. It is a rich soil ready prepared for the vigorous growth and spread of any of those destructive maladies that keep stalking about the Oriental world. The numerous trade connections of the town with places north and south and on the mainland necessitate a large fleet of great and small native craft. It is matter of history that these have been mainly instrumental in spreading the epidemics of cholera that have appeared on East Africa; but as things are, there is no manner of check to the introduction of epidemic disease, and no preparation of any kind to meet its possible sudden appearance and to arrest its spread. The commercial position of Zanzibar ought to render the health of the port of primary importance, but "sufficient unto the day is the evil thereof;" and there seems to be hardly a thought for any other consideration than the wealth of the port. Quarantine regulations have no existence, and it is believed they could not exist here under any circumstances, even if such regulations were less futile than is becoming more and more apparent concerning them. In a recent paragraph of *The Lancet* it is remarked that "the so-called 'quarantine' system at our colonial ports is a delusion and a mockery, . . . cruel and detrimental to commerce. . . . . . . Security against such epidemics being introduced along our waterways will depend, as security against them on our landways, upon the completeness and efficiency of the ordinary sanitary arrangements, rather than upon arrangements made to meet the exigency of the moment, and which at the best must be merely stop-gaps." It is in this particular, the entire absence of "ordinary sanitary arrangements," that Zanzibar is culpable and running a serious risk from year to year; and if anything so devastating as cholera should again find a footing in our midst, censure would be liberally awarded to the local authorities, and there would be a great noise in locking the stable after the horse was stolen. It is high time that something were done to place Zanzibar, as it deserves to be, in the front among trading ports; and that *something* must be in the shape of "a systematic sanitary inspection of all vessels immediately after arrival, and if any cases of contagious sickness are found, to remove them to a place provided for the purpose." These measures imply the services of a Port Surgeon and

an hospital having an efficient staff. It is believed the Sultan, whose co-opera-
tion is of course required in working out such a scheme, is so fully alive to the
commercially increasing value of his position, that any reasonable protective
measures would meet with his approval and support. It has to be said, however,
that the Arabs generally are slow to move in the way of progress, and they
vaguely hope that as their fate has been, so it will continue to be; and why
therefore interfere with its operations? Trouble and expense are lions in their
path.

In the above connection it is worthy of notice as a curious fact that an
order in Council decrees that all Bills of Health shall
Bills of Health. be issued and certified by the Consul-General, and that
no medical testimony is required as to the health of the town and port at stated
intervals. A Bill of Health seems to imply by its name that it is a medical
instrument,—medico-legal rather,—and that it ought to be issued as such, while
the Consul's seal and signature would give it the due impress of legal authority.
If the present course of issue must be adhered to *by order*, then at least a
formal certificate as to the health of the town and island should be called for
at stated periods for the information of the Consul-General and duly registered.
On the other hand, if this duty—certainly an anomalous one at present—were
left entirely in the hands of the medical officer, subject to the authority of the
Consul-General, the small fee charged on each Bill of Health would add in a
measure to the medical officer's emoluments.

The climate of Zanzibar does not merit the abusive terms commonly applied
to it. It is not a healthy one by any means, but it is
Climatology and Health. at the same time not so unhealthy as many persons
themselves contrive to make it. There is only a moderate rainfall during the
year, but a reference to the tables appended to this report will shew at once
that the climate is essentially a humid one. It is the constantly humid atmo-
sphere and the small amplitude of the mean temperature throughout the year
that render the climate so debilitating, and a healthy nervous system is always
more or less radically impaired by prolonged residence. There is not at any
time the high temperature registered at such places as Aden, Muscat, the
Persian Gulf generally, and Sind; nor does the minimum thermometer sink so
low as at these. The mean temperatures of February and March, the hottest
months of the year, are $83 \cdot 1°$ and $83 \cdot 4°$ Fahrenheit, and of July and August,
the coolest months, $77 \cdot 5°$ and $77 \cdot 7°$. So that the amplitude of the yearly
fluctuation is rather less than $6°$, while the percentage of saturation, taking
the averages of the months, ranges from 78 to $83 \cdot 2$. Moisture and heat are
the agencies that most highly favour decomposition, and where these are persistently at work in a densely populated locality, it is evident that sanitary pre-
cautions are of the utmost importance. The observations given in the appendix
are the result of daily recorded readings of various instruments for five conse-
cutive and unbroken years, and they perhaps give a fair average estimate of the
meteorological conditions affecting the climate of Zanzibar. Regarding the
exaggerated readings of the maximum thermometer for 1874, and the first four
months of 1875, and the range of the months and of the years affected thereby,
it is necessary to explain that the maximum and minimum thermometers' cage
had a faulty position, which, though perfect as regards shade and ventilation,
was under a piece of corrugated iron roofing at a distance of about 6 feet
from the cage. Circumstances at the time prevented this cage from having the
better exposure it has since occupied. The exaggerated readings have reference only to the points noticed. The minimum thermometer was not in any way
affected, and the mean daily readings have all been deduced from registering a
separate thermometer, having a position fulfilling all the requirements of accurate observation. In tabulating the averages of the months (B) and of the
years (C), in order to secure a fairer estimate of them, only the complete years
and the complete months have been taken into account. A foot-note explains
this where necessary. Some instruments were wanting for a while as shewn on
the records, but there are still three and a half years complete, even if it is
deemed necessary to set aside 1874 and the early part of 1875. It has not

been possible to give more than the general direction of the wind; and the amount of cloud and of evaporation is not recorded. The dew point temperature and the percentage of saturation have been worked out by using Mr. Glaisher's factors. Regarding evaporation, Parkes says : " For physicians the amount of evaporation is a very important point, not merely as influencing the moisture of the air abstractedly, but as affecting the evaporation from the skin and lungs." Yet he goes on to remark that " it is not easy to determine it experimentally, and no instrument is issued by the Army Medical Department. In a temperate climate like that of Europe, with a mean temperature of $52\frac{1}{4}°$, the annual evaporation is considered equal to a layer of water 37 inches thick; but within the tropics it varies from 80 to 100 inches, though it is said not much more than the half of this amount is to be found at Zanzibar. Evaporation does not go on unchecked, however, especially in the western districts of the island, for there is a rank luxuriance of protecting and absorbing vegetation requiring for its nourishment all the moisture that can be derived from a rainfall at no time excessive. The average annual rainfall of five years is only 61 inches, and without the presence of trees and grasses in abundance, the soil would not only be robbed of moisture, but its precious chemical ingredients would be decomposed and abstracted by the action of the solar rays. These conditions are no doubt prejudicial to health, but only where the growth of vegetation is natural and the soil uncultivated. Hardly any atmospheric condition is of more importance to Zanzibar than the rainfall. To raise and carry to maturity the food-crops of the island, the rainfall must not be excessive, nor must it come in sudden deluges. These would result in damage to crops already standing, and in more general destruction by washing away the thin coating of soil which is not in any place too abundant or rich for the plants committed to it. Comparing the recorded rainfalls of former years, 85 to 167 inches, as stated by Burton and Christie, with the results of the past five years, the average rainfall above given shews a decrease of one-fourth on the smaller of the two numbers quoted. Meteorologists recognise an intimate connection between the presence of trees and rainfall, and it is said that the rapid progress of tree-planting in the treeless tracts of the north-west of the United States at the present time suggests that climatic changes of an advantageous nature will be recorded in the next generation. Viewed in this light, it may be that the diminution of the rainfall of recent years at Zanzibar is due to the great destruction of trees over the whole island by the cyclone of 1872; and a sentence of Dr. Christie's on this subject is worth quoting here: " If the amount of rainfall depends in any degree on the number of trees on the island, then there must be a great decrease for many years to come, as the cyclone destroyed nearly all the large trees in the island." The illustration of the truth of this supposition is in the rainfalls of the past five years; but Dr. Christie left Zanzibar in the early part of 1874, and it is believed that since that time,—that is, from the beginning of 1874,—the only recorded rainfalls at Zanzibar are those herewith submitted. Unless, therefore, Dr. Christie is referring to the last half of 1872, after the cyclone, and to 1873, of which I can find no record, more recent observations do not bear him out in the statement that there " has been no decrease as yet in the rainfall, appearances being rather in the opposite direction." The average number of rainy days is 120—one-third of the year ; and only once in five years has the rainfall of 24 hours reached 4·74 inches. The greater rains fall in March, April, and May, with their maximum in April, shewing an average of 14·84 inches for that month ; the lesser rains are from mid-October to the end of the year, November and December giving an average each of 7·38 inches and 8·06 inches. The driest month is September, with 1 inch 86 cents of rain. The rains usually mark the change of the monsoons. The southerly winds in the west and east inclinations blow more or less steadily from the beginning of May to October, and the heavy rains of this monsoon reach Bombay towards the end of June. From the middle of December till about the middle of March the north-east monsoon is steady, veering round into due east in the afternoons. Taking the year as a whole, and all classes of the inhabitants, February and March shew themselves to be the healthiest months, and they are comparatively dry. This is equally true of the island and the mainland opposite, and towards the end of the north-east monsoon is considered the best time for visiting the coast. The unhealthy seasons are those immediately following the rains, and the Indian residents suffer most severely from May to July and even August,—that is, the months following the heavy rains when there is a steady lowering of the temperature. The cool months are looked forward to with delight by the European as something to be enjoyed; but care enough is not taken to guard against the sometimes rapid changes of temperature during these months, particularly after sunset, and hence it is that they become so productive of sickness. It is a common practice to seek the treacherous comfort of sleeping outside all night, or in a direct draught; but there are few who escape having to regret such an indulgence. The vitality—that is, the temperature—of the body in health is at its lowest ebb in the early morning between the hours of two and four; and then it is that the night air and the dews, which are often very heavy, sow the seeds of bad health in bowel complaints and fevers, particularly where there is a predisposition to such. Indeed, the seeds are already sown where a predisposition exists, and only the quickening agency is required for their growth. Relapses of fever invariably follow a *sudden* fall of temperature. Malarial poison takes time to shew itself, and a cold temperature will develop it. This is the explanation of certain so-called malarious hill sanitaria, where the low temperature has brought to light the disease, really acquired, though not shewn, either by residence in or by merely passing through a malarious district. Thus it is also that in temperate climates sudden cold causes relapses of ague in those who have been exposed abroad in hot climates to the influence of malaria; and this, I believe, is a sufficient explanation of the so-called " Zanzibar " or " Chill " Fever which Dr. Christie says " is not malarious, although it assumes the intermittent type." Few persons resident in the tropics escape contracting fever some time or other, and few places can be pointed out where malaria does not exist in some degree of activity; for heat, moisture, and decomposing vegetable matters are common and constant factors. Besides lowering of temperature, there are other determining causes of an attack of fever, such as over-exposure to the sun, catching a chill either from want of care when perspiring freely or after getting wet, over-eating and over-drinking, even under mental anxiety. But personal experience has shewn that in almost all cases of fever with well-marked intermissions there has been the history of possible exposure to malarial influence at the outset of the disease, and undoubtedly the virulence of the malarial poison is intensified by defective sanitation. Regarding *malaria* itself, whatever that may be, there is at the present day difference of opinion as to its conditions of activity. In some recent correspondence in *The Lancet* on this subject, one party attributes ague to " inhaling the odour of decaying vegetation;" while another, writing from a large experience, doubts " if malaria is ever caused by decaying vegetation," and considers " the most fruitful source of malarious fever to be exposure to the emanations arising from recently turned up virgin soil, or from ground from which the vegetation has recently been removed." This writer, in support of his opinion, based upon " twenty years' experience of tropical fevers," instances, among other facts, " the unhealthiness of the Assam tea gardens when the virgin forest is first cleared away;" and that in " rice-fields, so long as the rice is growing and the field is *covered with water*, there is no fear of malaria; but when the rice is cut and the ground begins to dry up, with no vegetation on it, then fever makes its appearance in the vicinity." He adds that, " to counteract in some measure the evil effects arising from the emanations from newly turned up soil, the ground should be freely sprinkled with dry lime, and, where feasible, beaten hard into what is called in the East *chunam*, or, better still, covered with turf. At the same time, vegetation should be encouraged to grow as rapidly as possible." The recommendation in the last sentence quoted requires to be more exactly defined. The Island of Pemba and some of the coast of the mainland are notoriously productive of intermittent fever among the British-Indian subjects; but whether the planting and harvesting seasons at those places have anything to do with the increase of fever, is not correctly ascertained. As has been already noticed, the rainy seasons are decidedly unhealthy, especially when the rains have ceased; and no doubt sudden falls of temperature during heavy rains and thunder-storms are sufficient to reproduce an attack of fever, independent of a rain-broken and moist soil acted on by a tropical sun. During five years, the Germans and then the Americans among

E

white residents have enjoyed the best health; and, excluding the numerous missionaries in this quarter, whose habits of life are in some points exceptional, the British residents have suffered rather more than the French from causes of sickness. The Germans and the French are large consumers of the lighter wines and beers; the Americans live moderately; while it is our notorious weakness as a nation to indulge freely in the strongest embodiments of alcohol. All follow active business lives. This luxury of life—ardent spirits—is selected for remark, because, all other things being equal, it is their free and constant use that aggravates tropical diseases, if it does not, indeed, directly predispose to them. Alcohol is both constructive and destructive: destructive directly and persistently in all states of health and in most cases of ordinary sickness; constructive only in acute specific diseases and in all cases where progressive tissue waste of the body would ultimately interfere with the natural functions of life but for the prompt and judicious supply of alcohol to arrest this tissue waste by substitution. The foul-smelling beach might be supposed to have an injurious effect upon the health of those whose houses are built quite close to it. Some have complained of headache, languor, and drowsiness when the smell has been very strong; but there is no evidence of any illness approaching a paroxysmal fever type, though in one or two cases a temporary hyper-action of the bowels has been referred to the low-tide beach as a cause. It may be with the Zanzibar beach, as in the singular case of the Singapore salt marshes, which set free large quantities of sulphuretted hydrogen, that "the regular tidal overflow, though it causes the development of much sulphuretted hydrogen, prevents the formation of malaria."

The food of the slaves and of the poorer classes consists of manioc, fruit, and salted shark. The salted shark is imported from Food. Muscat. The other articles are in great abundance in the island all the year round. Rice and meat are luxuries and rare. The manioc is eaten boiled, or it is split up, sun-dried, and pounded to flour to make cakes and a kind of gruel. Jack fruit is largely patronised and is considered nutritious. Much of the daily bread of the hard-working classes is to be had for sale on the streets, and many women combine the making and selling of these articles of food with the making of mats. Ground rice, stirred up in the proper proportions with cocoanut oil and a kind of treacle, is used to make the most common kind of street cake. Jowaree (known as Indian millet or Caffre corn) is also employed in the same way. It is either mixed with treacle only to a pasty consistence and sold in the shape of balls, or it is mixed with cocoanut oil and made into cakes. In this last form it is the common and almost only food of the Sheher Arabs, and one cake in the morning and another in the evening is said to be their daily allowance. One cake costs one pice, and the day's allowance weighs about one pound. These Shehers are a short well-set tribe, wiry and hard working, but very miserly in their habits of life. Some of them are possessed of much wealth. Other ordinary foods are sweet potatoes, groundnuts, heads of Indian corn roasted, and various kinds of fresh fish sometimes to be had in plenty. Fowls and butcher-meat are frequently used by the better class of natives who can afford to buy these things. The bullock and the goat are the animals killed for the usual meat supply, and they come from the mainland, chiefly from the ports north of Zanzibar. The camel and fat-tailed sheep come down to Zanzibar in numbers during the north-east monsoon. The camel is largely killed and eaten, and its flesh is preferred by the Arab tribes to all other kinds. It is cheaper, too, when it is in season. I am assured that an adult native at rest—that is, not employed in hard manual labour—can subsist and keep in good condition on one of the Sheher cakes noticed above, weighing half a pound and costing one pice, with a small cupful of coffee measuring rather more than an ounce, as a daily allowance for a considerable time. Exact experiment, however, is wanting to prove the accuracy of such a statement. The Indian subjects want for nothing in the way of food that they could have in their own country. Some of their food-grains are cultivated in the island and on the mainland, but the Hindoos especially are particular about what they eat, and large importations of the cereals, chiefly rice, come from different parts of India. The kind of rice prized by the Hindoo comes from the Malabar coast, and that coming from Kurrachee is said to be better than any other kind; it is of a reddish colour until ground, when it becomes quite white, and it is this kind that is chiefly eaten in sickness. Of vegetables, there is considerable variety growing in abundance in different parts of the island.

Regarding the slaves and the poorest classes of the natives, observation teaches that they

Dress.

". . . . . . want but little here below,
Nor want that little long."

A loin cloth of white or blue calico is the only garment of men and boys; females have the cloth longer and closely wrapped round the body under the arms, covering the breasts, but leaving the neck and shoulders bare; and, according to fashion, this cloth may be of various colours and patterns. Among those who are well to do, the waist cloth is of better material, and has usually a pattern worked into the lower border. This better garment is called a *kikoi*, the simple cloth arrangement noticed above being called an *ugno*. In addition to the *kikoi*, there is a long over-all garment of white calico like a night shirt; this is the *kanzu*, and is generally embroidered in a simple way about the neck, breast, and cuffs. The head is covered with a red woollen or white cotton cap, called a *kofia*, though the *kofia* is in its proper Arabic sense a large Syrian silk handkerchief worn as a head-dress: the red woollen cap is, properly speaking, the *tarboosh* without its usual blue silk tassel; and the white cotton cap is the *takiyeh*, worn under the *tarboosh*. Thus, the *kofia*, the *kanzu*, the *kikoi*, and ordinary sandals (*viatu*) on the feet, constitute the common dress of the male natives of Zanzibar, which would be the undress of the upper classes and Arabs. The fuller dress, in addition to this, consists of the *azamu*, or shawl wound round the waist and supporting the *jambia*, or short curved dagger always worn by the Muscat Arabs; the *joho*, or long, loose, open coat, often richly embroidered at the edges; and the *kilemba*, or turban, which is a kind of large handkerchief made at Muscat and worn twisted round the *kofia*. "Usually it is of fine blue and white cotton check, embroidered and fringed with a broad red border, with the ends hanging in unequal lengths over one shoulder. . . . . . The ruling family and grandees, however, have modified its vulgar folds, wearing it peaked in front and somewhat resembling a tiara." In addition to the long cloth worn by the native women, those who can afford it wear on the head an *ukaya*, a piece of blue calico or gauze with two long ends flowing out behind or rolled up and twisted round the portion that covers the head; this head portion is kept in position by a number of fine cords joined together to form a band passing under the chin, from which band hangs a silver ornament called *jebu*. The dress, common amongst the Arab and half-caste women, is thus given by Bishop Steere: "They wear trousers, *sornali*, a *kanzu* of coloured materials, and a *kofia* (cap) adorned with gold and spangles, or more commonly a silk handkerchief, *dusamali*, folded and fastened on the head so as to hide the hair. They also wear sometimes a *kisibao* (embroidered waistcoat), and nearly always a mask, *barakoa*. When they go out, they throw over all a large square of black silk, *lebwani*. On their feet they carry wooden clogs held by a button (*msuruake*) grasped between the toes." In the young of both sexes, and in adult males, the head is, as a rule, shaved. Women have their short and crisp "locks" often elaborately parted and plaited.

The employments of the natives are here, as elsewhere, as various as the requirements of daily life. Almost anything that is

Occupations.

wanted can be bought or can be made; and some things are found in Zanzibar that are not to be met with elsewhere. The daily life of the upper classes is described as "one monotonous round of prayer, coffee, sherbet, bathing, calls, and conversation." Those so employed are the owners of large *shambas* in the country, and of house property in the town, and their wealth is accumulated by others. The middle classes are engaged in buying and selling for themselves, or as agents and overseers for others. Some of the lower ranks find employment as masons, carpenters, blacksmiths, weavers, mat-makers, sailors, fishermen; while others, like the teeming slave population, are engaged as domestics or daily labourers. Hired slave gangs are the "horse-power" of Zanzibar, the young and old of both sexes being employed in connection with the various industries of the place. They work cargoes, pick and sort orchilla weed, sift and clean copal, wash cowries, dry hides, and are the general *hamalis* or porters of the town. These slaves are a happy-go-lucky race, although they sometimes lead hard enough lives; and they are fairly well treated by their masters only for the same reason that we ourselves at home well treat our horse or our cow,—they cost money, and their services, while in health and good condition, are valuable because productive. Indeed, one is safe in assert-ing that there is often far more affection for the horse and the cow, apart from their services, amongst ourselves than is to be found amongst East African slave-holders for their slaves.

Elephantiasis, affecting chiefly the legs and scrotum, and *lumbrici*, infesting
          the bowels, may almost be considered endemic diseases
Diseases.   in Zanzibar. But with these exceptions, the prevailing
diseases of the place are such as are more or less common to all tropical countries.

Fevers are very common, both intermittent and remittent. The remittent type is that more frequently met with, but in many cases the remissions are so little marked that the fever assumes more or less of a continued form and ends fatally with typhoid symptoms. All classes of the community suffer from some of the forms of fever, but the British-Indian subjects present the worst cases, and the very worst are those coming from the trading ports on the mainland. The natives blame the drinking-water for most of their ailments, and undoubt-edly waters such as have been described are fraught with the germs of disease. It is an old wide-spread belief that drinking the water of marshes generates malarious fevers, and it is not, perhaps, too much to suppose that the bad types of fever coming from the coast towns are as much due to the waters used for domestic purposes as to the particular situation of the towns themselves. In very many cases coming from the coast, and in others originating in the town, the temperature is never very high, but it is persistent and little impressed by the exhibition of quinine. The skin is sometimes burning hot, sometimes hot and clammy; occasional nausea and wandering pain in the bowels, which are irregu-lar, though mostly constipated; there are languor and loss of appetite; frontal and occipital headache with vertigo; a white furred tongue; and pinched and sallow countenance. These are the characteristics of a fever causing much debility among all classes of the Indian residents, because it is for a long time neglected, seeing that it does not altogether incapacitate for business. It is due almost entirely to the irritation caused by intestinal worms, and is usually got rid of by the free use of vermifuges, such as santonine, turpentine, and castor-oil, which expel sometimes very large collections of *lumbrici*. If the feverish state persists, it is now easily removed by the use of quinine in the first place, and then a course of iron or bitter tonics. Infantile remittents are very com-mon, and they kill a large number of the Indian children. They are almost always due to the presence of worms aggravating the troubles of dentition, and end fatally with coma and convulsions. There is often much culpable neglect on the part of the parents or attendants, until the case is hopeless. The severe remittents met with among Europeans have been contracted on the mainland, in exploring or shooting expeditions near the coast; and it is a usual thing to say that no European who has been so employed is to consider himself free from an attack of coast fever until a fortnight or three weeks have passed after his return to Zanzibar. In these remittents there is usually much irritability of stomach with bilious vomiting, and the *back-pain* is a well-marked symptom in nearly all cases. One patient described it as such that he kept tossing uneasily from one position in bed to another in seeking to find out the particular bone of the spine that was not broken. Others complain of a *cutting* pain radiating from near the union of the lumbar and dorsal vertebræ towards both sides and stopping on a vertical line with the nipples. There is general muscular pain besides, and the calves of the legs are frequently referred to as the seat of much pain. It would seem to be more in the fibrous structures that the malarial poison is active, for the larger joints are often complained of, and the more frequent pain in the back of the legs may be rather in the large fibrous expansion from the heel to the gastrocnemius muscle than in the muscle itself. Owing to an insanitary condition of dwelling or neighbourhood, the original malarial characters of a fever may be departed from, and typhoid symptoms take their place. There is a rapid failing of the vital powers attended by a bilious or hæmorrhagic diarrhœa. This may be called the typho-malarial type, and I suspect many of the worst cases of fever amongst the native races belong to this class. Their early features are mostly unknown, for assistance is sought only in their last and fatal stage; and the circumstances attending the treatment of such cases, without the system of an hospital, admit only of attention to therapeutic measures. Only in one case, that of a European, have I been able to see typhoid symptoms clearly established, except as regards the characteristic spots which were doubtful; and so persistent and uniform were the enteric features during life, that, but for the true initial malarial stage, the case would have been set down as one of typhoid (enteric) fever. There was no *post-mortem* examination to support the diagnosis.

Enlargements of the spleen are very common, and to an enormous size often in quite young children. Some mothers (British-Indian) have declared to me that their babies have been born with "a large lump in the left side." Medicines in such cases are not of much permanent benefit, and only a change to their native country is productive of good. Poverty often stands in the way.

The uncomplicated fever of the town of Zanzibar is of a mild character, but it is none the less debilitating when often repeated. Its first approaches, due as a rule in the new comer to various kinds of indiscretion, are not suffi-ciently heeded. It is a mistake made by some, either from necessity or choice, to think that this fever can be "worked" or "walked" away, and that indifference to its warnings is the best remedy. The fever no doubt quits,—that is, its period passes for the time, but its elements are still present though dormant; it returns, and returns again, to be treated with the same defiance, until the grand explo-sion comes, and the fever is conqueror at last. Now has arrived the time when by resolute measures the fever has to be dealt with and removed, and the task is not so easy as it would have been at first. It is the neglected beginnings that do mischief; they lead to much chronic bad health, and often to costly invalid-ings. The first trifling fever of the new arrival taken proper notice of may, in its weakness, be so roughly handled that it will quit for good; but treated as a guest ignorant that he is not made quite welcome, the visits will be repeated until they become obnoxious as those of an enemy who has to be turned out by force—"an enemy," says a writer on West Indian fevers, "equally skilled in retreat as in attack, and one whose complete rout need never be expected." Paying due attention to the various secretions, most cases of even severe un-complicated malarious fevers will yield to rest, quinine, and a suitable dietary; and experience teaches that one or two large doses of quinine are more effec-tual and more economical than many small doses spread over days at regular intervals. Alcohol in some of its forms is a valuable auxiliary, and often quite indispensable as a food rather than a medicine. It is necessary to meet the rapid waste caused by prolonged fevers in debilitated constitutions.

Diarrhœa and *dysentery* are frequent, and are greatly due to the unclean habits of the people and to the water they drink. The presence of *lumbrici* in the intestinal tract is a common cause. In Europeans they are caused by injudicious exposure of the body to draughts and changes of temperature, and also by too free indulgence in over-ripe and unripe fruits. Not long ago some cases of diarrhœa and dysentery in H. M. S. *London* were traced to the eating of pine-apples, and in consequence the men were forbidden to use that fruit.

Catarrhs are common, as might be expected where the temperature is variable and liable to sudden changes. During February and March of 1877, there was a widespread *influenza* in the town with considerable pyrexia. About August and September, mild cases of *hooping-cough* are heard in the streets among the native children.

Diseases of the heart and *general circulation* are seldom met with. Palpi-tations are not infrequent, but they are functional only. The coolies who do the heavy porterage of the town are believed to be a short-lived class of men; when they are at work, the strain on their hearts is continuous and must be severe, and it is not improbable that many of them succumb to the effects of hypertrophy and dilatation of that organ.

Sunstroke and *heat apoplexy* are not often met with, except in the case of the crews of merchant vessels in the harbour.

F

Among *intestinal worms*, the lumbricus is the most prevalent kind. The thread-worm and the tape-worm are met with from time to time, the tape-worm chiefly amongst the German residents.

Venereal diseases are widespread and are met with in all their varieties. Extensive chancres and their constitutional effects are frequently treated by salivation with some of the crude preparations of mercury to be had in the bazar, and it is too often the case that the cure becomes, if possible, worse than the disease. There is, of course, on control of these diseases, and they have their own free course. It is said that when a woman is discovered with the disease by her friends, she is at once taken charge of. As often as necessary, she is taken to the beach or other convenient spot, and after the parts have been thoroughly washed with sand and water, even to the effusion of blood, the sores are liberally supplied with sulphate of copper in powder or solution. The pain of such a practice must be extreme, but I am informed this local treatment is as thoroughly successful as it is vigorous and in earnest. It is singular that syphilitic sequelæ are so seldom seen among the native women. It is, perhaps, because they do not come forward for treatment as the men do. The morals of the native population are at a very low ebb, and it seems a strange inconsistency that their native modesty of outward behaviour should be so unaffected and almost refined.

Rheumatism is very common, and no doubt much of it has its origin in the malarial poison and in long-established gonorrhœas.

Hydrocele is so common among all classes that the tapping of one is almost as often called for as the drawing of a tooth. Not many patients will submit to the radical cure by injecting pure tincture of iodine ; they dread the subsequent pain of the injection, and the necessary confinement to the house for a few days is objectionable. So long as they can, with little pain, get rid of the collection of fluid and can conduct their daily duties as usual, they are quite ready to appear again when necessary to have the operation repeated.

Elephantiasis arabum affects all classes of the natives, high and low, rich and poor, and the residents from India are not excepted. Hydrocele and slight enlargements of the scrotum are found amongst the white residents, chiefly the Germans ; but in no case has elephantiasis in any of its forms made its appearance. It is essentially a blood disease expressing itself through the lymphatic system and in selected parts of the body. Most frequently the lower extremities below the knees aret he seat of the disease, one or both, mostly one leg only, and that the left. The skin of the penis and scrotum is also enormously hypertrophied in many cases, and the parts cause great inconvenience from their weight and great bulk. Only amputation of the hypertrophied portion is of any use when the scrotum is the seat of the disease, although many of the affected British-Indian subjects get rid of the disease entirely if they leave Zanzibar for their own country when the disease is in its early stage. Return to Zanzibar, however, most certainly brings back the disease. Not a few persons of both sexes are to be seen with both legs affected, but ordinary locomotion is not impeded ; two or three cases shew the upper extremities enlarged, but in no case these only—there has been long-standing hypertrophy of the legs. One interesting case (briefly recorded in *The Indian Medical Gazette* for March 1876) shews the disease in both legs, one of which is of very great bulk, in one arm, and in one breast ; the woman says she is otherwise unaffected. The disease when seated in the extremities may be looked upon as generally incurable. Good results are recorded as derived from prolonged elevation of the member, mercurial infrictions, and careful bandaging. Humid and hot climates are considered favourable to the development of the disease where the special dyscrasy is present. Hebra says, " Climate and the physical condition of the soil (the tropics, sea-coasts, low islands) have been considered . . . potential." The earliest age was about twelve years in a case where there was considerable hypertrophy of both legs. The boy, an African, could not remember when his legs began to grow large ; but he said he was a frequent sufferer from sharp fevers.

Ophthalmia and *corneal ulcerations* are rather prevalent. They have much to do with the unclean ways of the people, and they are of course aggravated by the heat and the dust and the intense glare of the place.

Skin diseases are also common, but seldom recognisable. They are usually the products of filth and poverty. The same conditions are to blame for the great frequency of ulcers and phlegmonous abscesses, affecting chiefly the lower extremities.

Epidemic diseases.—During the last five years no case of cholera has been heard of in the town; and not a single case of small-pox has come up for treatment. On one or two occasions the approach of small-pox from Madagascar *viâ* the coast of the mainland was reported; and although convalescents from the disease have been seen in the streets, it has never spread. Not long ago one or two cases were reported among the labourers on the English Mission plantation, but with these the disease seems to have died out.

Injuries are common enough, mostly in the form of stabs, sword cuts, and gunshot wounds. This is not to be wondered at, when almost every man and boy one meets carries a gun or a sword, a spear or a dagger, or it may be only the ordinary sheath knife, at the waist. Provocation meets with retribution on the spot. Large and deep wounds, and even dangerous-looking stabs, are readily recovered from, while a small insignificant ulcer is a tedious thing to cure. The *accidents* seen require no special mention.

It is only when the probable advent of small-pox occupies the minds of the people that they clamour for vaccination. At
Vaccination.
other times they refuse to accept it as a favour. When the operation has been done successfully, if the child be that of a Mahommedan, it is quite impossible to get permission to remove lymph from the arm; and so strong is prejudice or superstition, that the vesicles are wilfully destroyed, and of course the lymph originally expended dies with the particular operation. Vaccination has not therefore made steady progress in the town. The European children have been protected; and fortunately there has been some fresh lymph at hand to spread over the batches of captured slaves that have been landed from time to time, those at least to whom local British protection has been given. Lymph stored in tubes is found to deteriorate rapidly, and there is always some difficulty in starting a fresh supply in an emergency. Aden is the nearest point of supply, but there is only monthly communication with that station.

The practice of opium-eating is prevalent amongst the Khojahs. Some Banyans, too, have adopted the habit. Some residents
Opium-eating.
here have been using the drug for twenty or thirty years; and one old man, recently dead, did not once omit his daily allowance for the long period of forty years. Regular consumers take about four or five grains weight of the drug sold in the bazars in two doses, morning and evening; its use is certainly compatible with long life, and in very many cases there is a remarkable immunity from exhausting diseases. It is possible to break off the habit, but the attempt is attended with an amount of distress that is said to be utterly unbearable, and the habit is taken up again as the only escape from impending death. Dr. Dudgeon, of Pekin, says that "large numbers die annually in the prisons of China from deprivation of the drug, being almost wholly carried off by diarrhœa and dysentery—diseases which prove quite intractable in opium-smokers." The testimony of Wilberforce to the value of the drug in his own person is a curious and interesting one. He is said to have suffered greatly (about the age of thirty) from what was called an entire decay of all the vital functions. Consultation of chief physicians said that "he had not stamina to last a fortnight," and he was "decently dismissed to the Bath waters." Contrary to all expectations, he was visibly gaining strength at Bath. His returning health was in great measure the effect of a sparing use of opium— a medicine which even Dr. Pitcairne's authority could scarcely make him use. As a stimulant, he never knew its effect, nor in twenty years did he ever increase the dose. "If I take," he would often say, "but a single glass of wine I can feel its effect; but I never know by my feelings when I have taken my medicine." Its intermission was at once followed by the recurrence of disorder. (*Life of Wilberforce.*)

The natural productions met with in Zanzibar that supply the export market
Natural Trade Productions.
are ivory, gum copal, cloves, semsem, red pepper, cocoanuts, cocoanut oil, the dried cocoanut (copra),

orchilla weed, india-rubber, hides, coir rope, shells, a kind of ebony, and Zanzibar rafters. Ivory comes from the interior of Africa in exchange for cotton, brass and iron wire, and beads. Copal is dug out of the ground, at no great depth, a few miles inland from the coast in the Dar-es-Salaam district, a little to the south of Zanzibar, on the mainland. On the authority of Dr. Kirk, Her Majesty's Political Agent at Zanzibar, the scientific name of the true copal tree is *Trachylobium hornemannianum* (Hayne). The Island of Zanzibar yields an inferior quality of the gum in small quantity. Cloves have been cultivated here for about fifty years: the largest plantations are on the Island of Pemba and in the hands of the Arabs chiefly. The semsem of commerce is the seeds of *Sesamum indicum*, extensively grown on the mainland about Lamoo, north of Zanzibar. Sesamum, jinjili, or til oil, so well known throughout India, is expressed from these seeds. Orchilla weed comes down in large quantities from the Galla and Somali coasts in the north; and india-rubber comes from the copal districts, but farther inland. Hides are furnished by the Galla and Somali countries, by the Comoro Islands and Madagascar. The species of ebony brought from the interior for export is said not to belong to a large-sized tree; it is the *Dalbergia melanoxylon*, which produces a beautifully variegated wood with black and white streaks. East Indian ebony is the heartwood (abnoos) of the *Diospyros melanoxylon*—a much more easily worked wood, according to the Indian carpenters here, than the African product. The Zanzibar rafter (boriti) is the red mangrove (*Bruguiera cylindrica*) cut down in large quantities on the mainland, and brought over for local use and export; the white species is the *Avicennia tomentosa*, used only for fuel in lime-burning.

The principal fruit trees and plants are the orange of two or three kinds, bitter and sweet, and in season twice a year; the lemon and the lime; the shaddock or pummelo (*Citrus decumana*); the plantain, or banana, all the year round; a large and a small variety of mango, in season twice a year (*Mangifera indica*); the pine-apple (*Bromelia ananas*), in many places growing wild and to be had at any time; the papaw tree (*Carica papaya*); the guava (*Psidium pyriferum*); cashew-nut (*Anacardium occidentale*): the kernel of the nut which hangs at the end of the fruit outside, and is kidney-shaped, when roasted, is very pleasant, but considered astringent; a very acrid juice between the double shell covering the kernel will at once raise a blister if applied to the skin. The cocoanut tree is of two kinds,—the common one and a dwarf species known here as the Pemba cocoanut; the fruit of the latter is large and smooth, of a pinkish yellow when ripe, and without the fibrous outer covering of the common cocoaunt; it gives very little oil, but supplies a refreshing drink in hot weather. Custard-apple is also of two kinds, *Anonna reticulata* and *A. squamosa;* and the pomegranate (*Punica granatum*) is common all over the island, but of an inferior quality and little used. Fruits specially cultivated in the Arab plantations are grapes, the rose-apple (*Eugenia jambosa*), the fig, the leichee (*Nephelium* (or *Scytalia*) *litchi*), the loquat* (*Eriobotrya japonica*), and the "doriyan," an offensive-smelling fruit from the *Durio zibethinus*. The jack tree (*Artocarpus integrifolia*) is itself common in the island. The Arabs prize the "doriyan" as a delicacy, and not long ago a good-sized specimen of the fruit cost one rupee. Among the fruits eaten by the poorer classes is the jack fruit (*phunus* of India, called in Swahili *finessi*); the fleshy part is eaten uncooked, and the seeds either roasted or boiled. There is also the *kunāzi* or Indian bher fruit (*Ziziphus jujuba*), which tastes like a crab-apple and is astringent; its wood is extremely tough, and it is said a fine gum-lac can be produced from the tree. It is especially cultivated by Mussulmans round their tombs, and the Arab dead are said to be washed with an infusion of the leaves. Another tree is the *zambaran*, the fruit of which, not unlike a damson, is also edible and astringent; it is the *jamoon* of India (*Eugenia jambulana* or *Syzygium jambulanum*), and its wood is used for lining wells, being very durable under water. The flat reticulated nut of the *kwemwé†* tree (a climber?) is roasted and eaten; it is said to yield a small quantity of bland oil. The reddish pulp of the *Tamarindus indicus*, which is common, is laxative and makes a cooling refrigerent drink in fevers.

Vegetable Life.

---

* Very rare.   † *Telfaria pedata.*

The calabash or baoba (*Adamsonia digitata*) is a common tree in the island; the pulp of its fruit is also eaten, and the fruit itself dried is used as a " bucket " in dip-wells,—two holes, each about an inch square, being made near the top of the shell, and its contents cleared out by setting fire to them. Besides those mentioned, there are few other trees. There are two species of *Ficus*, the peepul (*Ficus religiosa*) flourishing near the Hindu idol-houses; there are no " temples " as these are understood in India. The white silk cotton tree (*Eriodendron anfractuosum*) grows in the interior of the island; and the Malay almond tree (*Terminalia catappa*) is here and there met with in the town; it is called *beedam* by the Banyans, who use its broad firm leaves as platters for their food; one man is said to require six or eight of these leaves for his daily use, and they are stitched together to the required size and thrown away when the food has been eaten; the wood is said to be useless, and, although the ripe fruit is sometimes eaten off the tree, it is believed to cause fever " through the bowels." There are a few specimens of the date palm (*Phœnix dactylifera*) and of the palm-oil tree (*Elœeis guineensis*); and the Indian neem (*Azadirachta indica*) is seen to flourish. The nutmeg grows to perfection in the Sultan's shambas. Some of the common vegetables in use are the cucumber, a kind of vegetable marrow, the water-melon, sweet potato, yam (*Dioscorea alata*), brinjal or egg plant (*Solanum melongeno*), bhendi or edible hibiscus (*Abelmoschus* or *Hibiscus esculentus*), tomato (*Lycopersicon esculentum*), *baazi* of Zanzibar, the lequme (or its peas rather) of *Cajanus indicus*, or toor dhall of the Deccan. The vegetables in particular favour with the Banyans are *mooree*, a species of fennel, probably *Fœniculum panmorium; meethee-bhajee,* leaves of *Amarantus oleracens*, eaten as spinach or put into curries; and *kureela*, a creeper (*Momordica charantia*) sown at the beginning of the rains. Ginger grows on the island, but only in quantity sufficient for private use; the chief supply comes from Madagascar and the coast, and also from Bombay, the last being the best. Cinnamon is cultivated, but more for ornament than use. Cabbages, lettuce, and radishes are well grown at the French Mission at Bagamoyo, on the mainland opposite.

The animals found on the island are not in great number. A small but destructive leopard is met with in the interior, where a few striped pigs enjoy their freedom. Two kinds of civet cat are found, the large *ngawa* (*Viverra civetta*) and the small weasel-like *fungo* (*Viverra genetta*). Both, especially the former, are kept in confinement by the Arabs for the sake of their peculiar secretion, which is collected at regular intervals. Two species of the mungoose exist, one brown and vicious, the other striped and tameable. Bats are not in great variety; a large brownish-furred one frequents the mango trees, and a small smooth-skinned species lodges in the roofs of houses. There are several kinds of monkey, and the monkey-like *galago* (komba) is plentiful in the shambas, occupying the cocoanut trees, which they tap for the toddy. A kind of monkey called here *mbega*, with long black hair, white about the shoulders, is said to be found in the island, but it is chiefly on the mainland and towards the Masai country that they abound. There is a handsome small gazelle in the island and on the mainland; it is snared in great numbers for the sake of its skin. Pariah dogs and brown kites are, as elsewhere, the useful scavengers of the place; and " a fine large fish-hawk . . . . . . haunts the island and the coast." The Java sparrow, introduced about fifty years ago, is the sparrow of the town, and builds up every ventilating hole they can discover. White-breasted crows there are in the plantations, but they rarely visit the town. The grey red-tailed parrot, common as a pet, comes chiefly from Manyema land in the interior of Africa. Songsters and beautifully plumaged birds are in great variety; and the marshes and the sea-coast have their complement of snipes and wild-duck, sandpipers, cranes, and gulls. A blue pigeon frequents the islands in the harbour. Iguanas are common, and the natives have a great dislike to them, and also to the beautiful harmless chameleon. Snakes and lizards are not very troublesome, and are rarely met with. A small foot-and-a-half snake, blackish-brown above, greyish-white below, with a flat head, was killed when seen crossing a road in the country; the natives passing at the time declared it was a most deadly snake, and gave it a wide berth, even when almost dead. Pythons have been found lurking about houses in the country, particularly where fowls are handy.

G

One brought into town recently from the country-house of an Arab measured nearly 10 feet. Scorpions are few, but centipedes and millepedes often turn up unexpectedly, particularly in rainy weather. Rats and mice, cockroaches, spiders, black and white ants, and mosquitoes, infest most houses. Butterflies and moths are various, some of them very beautiful. Among beetles, the most destructive-looking individual is the rhinoceros beetle, short and broad, with the characteristic horn on the head; is destructive of the young coeoanut tree. Camels, donkeys, horses, bullocks, sheep, goats, are all imported. The domestic fowl is small and unsavoury. At the mouths of the rivers on the mainland are hippopotami and crocodiles; the lion, leopard, buffalo, giraffe, zebra, and various antelope are met with farther inland, while away towards the remote interior are the haunts of the elephant and rhinoceros.

The Arabs are particularly attached to their own methods of treating disease, and among them European therapeutics do not progress rapidly. The Indian subjects, too, have their own medicines, which they use in ordinary complaints, and there is hardly any of the bazar medicines of India that are not to be had in Zanzibar. Again, the natives of the soil have a rude system of "doctoring," mixed up with the fetish belief in their *waganga*, or medicine men. Only a few of the native Indian drugs have distinct local names. The local name is often only a corruption of the name as used by the Indian settlers. The *dawa-ya-miti* of Zanzibar is the Indian choob-chinee (*Smilax china*), the rhizome of which is much used in making infusions for the cure of rheumatisms and general debility; the meaning of the local name is simply "the medicine of wood." Catechu, called in Swahili *katu*, and in Guzerati *kathho*, is chewed with the betel-leaf chiefly by women; men do not use it much in this way because it is "cooling." Rubbed up with sulphate of copper (*mrututu*) and yolk of egg, it is a common application to chancres.

'Mwango: the leaves—obovate, bright, and smooth—are boiled in water; the decoction is used as a wash in skin diseases. It is doubtful if this is the ringworm bush (*Cassia alata*).

Sâātar: the small leaves of pennyroyal (*Meutha pulegium*), a cold infusion of which is used in dyspepsias. The leaves come from Muscat and the Persian Gulf. Some prefer the hot infusion, drinking it like tea; others chew the leaves, or pound the leaves into a powder, having dried them well, and take a few grains morning and evening washed down with water.

Datura (alba) grows wild on rubbish heaps; a small portion of the leaf is often added by bhang drinkers to their potion to counteract the stage of excitement and to soothe to sleep.

Mūrū (Swah.), *Mŭrrh* (Arab.), is not found in Indian bazars; it comes from Makulla and Arabia generally; it is a compound medicine in the form of a small black cone; this is rubbed down on an earthen plate in water to the consistence of gruel, and taken as a drink for flatulence and dyspepsia; it is given to children very commonly; and internally and externally it is taken to allay the severe pain of orchitis.

Shabiri: copper-foil, cut into pieces about an inch or more square and spread over the chest and back at intervals for cough and general pains in the chest; in one case that came up for further treatment, two dozen of these patches were counted both before and behind. Is this a counter-irritant treatment by a chemical process?

Komwe :* a large climbing plant; the leaves are steeped in water for some time; they are then removed from the water and are themselves subjected to pressure; the water expressed is said to be a useful drink in cases of spleen; the root, treated much in the same way, yields a medicine used internally in cases of hydrocele.

Kwemwé :† another climbing plant; its reticulated seeds rubbed down in a little water are used in treating children for intestinal worms. Its root is employed as in the preceding for hydrocele.

Kanyé: a wax-like substance which comes from the mainland in moulds covered by an unknown leaf; this substance is probably the product of a species of Bassia. It is melted and rubbed into sprains and bruises.

---

* *Cæsalpinia bonducella* (Bon'ducnut).   † *Telfaria pedata*.

There is no civil hospital at Zanzibar, and no jail requiring, or rather per-
mitting, medical supervision. The Civil Surgeon's
The Civil Surgeoncy. duties are accordingly limited to professional attend-
ance on the officers and subordinates of the Political Agency, to the examination of such medico-legal cases as may from time to time come before court,
and to the medical care of the sick slaves that are frequently landed from
captured dhows. The dispensary is little better than a "godown" of the
Surgeon's house, roughly fitted for the purpose; but there is no accommodation
whatever for an in-patient, and but little convenience for the requirements of
ordinary out-patient practice.

There is hardly a greater public want in Zanzibar than that of a well-
appointed hospital, and one on a large scale would, it is believed, soon be
well occupied. The sick poor of the town are in great numbers, and their only
refuge at present is the streets. Private attempts in this direction have been
made, and so far the French Roman Catholic Mission has been successful in
opening wards for the convenience of all who care to avail themselves of them
in sickness. These wards are under the immediate control of the Mother
Superior of the Mission, assisted by several Sisters, and, although as yet incom-
plete with regard to the accessories of an hospital, they have already on many
occasions proved of service, particularly to seamen and strangers. This
hospital is in an airy position on the sea-beach looking south-west, and
it is well built. It was opened to the public about a year and a half ago,
on the 15th September 1877. It has a graduated liberal scale of daily
charges for those patients who can and are willing to pay. The English
Universities' Mission has also done something towards establishing a free
hospital; but at the present time, and from unavoidable causes, its accommodation is limited and hardly more than is necessary for the convenience of its
own members. This Mission does not, however, lose sight of such an institution
on a suitable scale when some of its present costly agencies of mission work
have a firmer footing and become more or less self-sustaining. But a public
free hospital ought to be a public gift. The providing of all that contributes to
the care and treatment of the sick poor of any community is an obligation
resting on those who are favoured with the good things of the world. In
Zanzibar the means abound in plenty, and only the grace of charity is needed to
put them in circulation. A public hospital might take a fitting place in the
programme of improvements set afoot by His Highness the Sultan, and
perhaps if the matter were fairly represented to him, he would be willing to
divert a portion of his generous liberality into this other channel of so much
good. Zanzibar is surely in a position to compete with Muscat, where His
Highness Seyed Toorkee "generously placed at the disposal of Her Britannic
Majesty's Consul and the Civil Surgeon the upper storey of a large house
formerly used as a family residence, free of rent, and with the permission of
Government it has been occupied since October 1873 as a hospital." The
hospital establishment at Muscat in 1875 consisted of a first class Hospital
Assistant, a hospital peon, and a night watchman. Contrast with this the position
of the Civil Surgeon at Zanzibar, even without a hospital, but with medicines,
instruments, &c., in charge, and dispensing to perform. In November of 1877,
an allowance of eleven rupees per mensem for a dispensary servant was
sanctioned by Government, but previous to that time,—that is, for a period of
four years,—the Civil Surgeon had to disburse from his own funds the pay of a
servant to keep the dispensary clean, &c. For a hospital, some good sites
already built on could be pointed out, and the buildings themselves would
require only necessary alterations for the purpose. If no place could be got on
the sea front, the house in the town of Hamed Abdullah bin Shakhsee would make
an admirable hospital. The purchase value would no doubt be great, but not
necessarily an insuperable difficulty; and Government, by lending some support
to the foundation of such an institution, would enlist the sympathy and support
of the Sultan himself. A hospital needs only to be opened to gather into it a
large and interesting sick population; and there is scope for much good
professional work in the systematic study of local diseases, to do which, however,
a well-organised hospital is a necessity.

Prisoners also deserve better consideration than it is possible to give them
in the present state of things. The Arab Fort has already been referred to. It

is the only jail in Zanzibar for all classes of the population, black and white, and one hears it sometimes dignified with the name of State Prison. Certainly it is not often a white man has to be confined in this place, yet refractory seamen do contrive sometimes to lose their liberty. It is difficult to learn how things are conducted within the Fort walls; accounts vary, but none are satisfactory. It seems at all events clear that any place employed for the confinement of British or British-Indian subjects ought to be at all times free and open to official supervision, and at least one daily visit of the medical officer ought to be made while British subjects are prisoners. The caste scruples of our Indian fellow-subjects would be thus carefully protected, and complaints would be heard and attended to. At present there is much conservatism in connection with the Fort; its internal economy is a mystery, the revealing of which is jealously guarded from too inquisitive eyes. An occasional necessary visit on duty, and armed with official authority, is usually attended with difficulty and some delay before entry is effected; and a careful Arab or half-caste escort prevents one's curiosity from making unnecessary excursions or investigations inside the walls. Perhaps there are important State reasons for so much care, or it may be only Arab jealousy and prejudice. Remonstrance is useless, and so too is the presented written authority of the Political Agent; the pleasure of the Sultan's Fort attendants has to be waited upon, and the importance of the permission granted is as ludicrous as it is sometimes offensive. The Sultan himself is said to exercise much leniency,—at times undue leniency,—towards offenders committed to the Fort. His own subjects, and such others as are specially recommended for the treatment, are linked neck to neck as labour-gangs and turned into the streets as occasion requires to do the work of scavengers and wheelbarrows. It is, of course, a great degradation to a British-Indian subject to be chained to a lot of ruffianly-looking Africans, but only an exceptional offence would merit such exceptional punishment. In the case of the Hindus, even a heavy fine, when such is admitted as an alternative in the awarded punishment, is gladly paid (by subscription among co-religionists, if that is necessary) in order to escape the horrors associated with imprisonment in the Fort. Sometimes, however, there is no alternative of fine, and even with the Hindu the law must be allowed to take its free course. If difficulties stand in the way of making reasonable arrangements with the Fort authorities for the due care and supervision of our own prisoners, independent measures ought to be taken to meet the case. The cells of H. M. S. *London* might become available for seamen, and for others the Government property known as the Jail Building might be employed as origin-ally intended. It is at present occupied by the Parsee clerks of the Consulate, some of the rooms on the ground floor having rubbish of various kinds stored away in them or are empty. This building was reported upon in 1874 as suit-able for a small jail and hospital, but the subject was never taken up. The subject of prison discipline is occupying public attention at home at the present day, for criminals are not looked upon as altogether outcasts even when under-going imprisonment, and much thought and labour are expended in connection with their legitimate treatment. "We have no foolish sentiment towards the criminal classes. . . . By all means let us punish criminals to the full extent of their physical endurance, but not beyond; and in order to do this safely, it will be necessary to keep a constant watch over each individual prisoner, and regulate his task and diet accordingly ;. . . . . . and we would further urge the necessity, in all cases where punishment is inflicted in prison for idleness or obstinacy, that careful thermometric records of the prisoner's temperature should be taken, lest the supposed idleness be found too late to be due to pneumonia or tuberculosis." (*Lancet.*) We have always ranked high in the estimation of other nations for the care bestowed upon our prison population; and a lesson of the same kind would certainly not be without its value to the Arab authorities at Zanzibar. That progress in the place is the order of the day is manifest on all hands; but it seems as if at some points its march were wanting in control and wise direction. Zanzibar bids fair to occupy a far higher platform of importance than it has ever before reached; and to hold this position securely, works and institutions of public usefulness must have their proper place in the constitution of the town. Among those requiring first consideration are a sufficient and continuous supply of pure wholesome water for the use of the town; a properly endowed hospital open to all who have a legitimate claim to charity; a jail that need not be " a place whose very name should develop the goose-skin," but one having some at least of the humanities attached to it ; and last, though perhaps not least in the commercial interests of the town, an efficient pier or jetty to bridge over the difficulties that presently exist in connection with the working of cargoes.

Without the medical charge of a hospital and jail, and the health of the port to look after, the Civil Surgeon's duties are neither very heavy nor very important ; and only the practice to be had in the town keeps alive professional interest. The present duties may, without difficulty, be handed over to a private local practitioner ; and the remarks not along ago made by Mr. Gathorne Hardy (now Lord Cranbrook) in his speech on the Army Estimates, though directed to the military service, seem equally applicable to the Zanzibar Civil Surgeoncy. With regard to " the employment of civil practitioners in certain circumstances," he said, " no doubt in some instances it is thought advisable to employ civil practitioners, because at stations where there is only a very small detachment, it would be absurd to place a military medical man there, and a civilian on the spot often likes to add to his fees by such employment as we can give him." It is to be hoped, however, that the Zanzibar medical appointment may not be allowed to decline, and that the place is deserving of more complete medical aid by Government no one acquainted with it will deny. The field is a large one, medical and surgical, and the future may yet see the station, not as an insufficiently administered second class surgeoncy, but as one of the first class, fully equipped, and in thorough working order.

JOHN ROBB, M.D.,
Surgeon, Her Majesty's Bombay Army,
Civil Surgeon at Zanzibar.

Zanzibar, East Africa,
4th March 1879.

A.

Results of Meteorological Observations taken at Zanzibar, East Africa.

Latitude 6° 9' 40" S., Longitude 39° 14' 20" E.
Thermometers about 27 feet above mean tide-level.
Rain Gauge   ,,   44   ,,   ,,   ,,   ,,

| 1874. | THERMOMETER | | | | | | | SOLAR RADIATION. | | BAROMETER. | HYGROMETER. | | | RAIN. | | | Prevailing winds. |
	Maximum.	Minimum.	Range of month.	Mean Maximum.	Mean Minimum.	Mean Daily range.	Mean Daily temperature.	Maximum.	Mean.	Mean corrected and reduced.	Degree of humidity. Saturation = 100.	Mean Temperature of evaporation.	Mean Temperature of dew point.	Number of rainy days, one cent. and above.	Total fall (inches, cents.).	Greatest fall in 24 hours.	
January	89.0	76.0	13.0	86.8	77.6	9.2	82.3				83	76.8	74.4	6	0.34	0.26	
February	91.5	72.0	19.5	88.5	78.4	10.1	82.8				81	76.9	74.2	7	3.34	.270	
March	92.5	73.0	19.5	88.9	78.8	10.1	83.9				81	78.1	75.5	10	6.10	2.45	
April	91.5	71.5	20.0	85.3	76.4	8.9	82.5				85	77.8	75.9	16	15.18	3.74	
May	88.0	71.5	16.5	84.6	74.6	10.0	80.3				79	74.2	71.3	11	4.90	2.04	
June	91.7	72.0	19.7	84.6	73.8	10.8	79.2				82	73.7	71.3	4	1.61	0.99	
July	93.0	70.0	23.0	83.9	72.3	11.6	77.6				80	71.8	69.1	4	1.09	0.78	
August	84.2	69.0	15.2	82.6	71.8	11.6	77.3				83	73.1	69.8	9	0.67	0.23	
September	85.0	71.0	14.0	83.3	72.3	11.0	78.2				84	73.0	70.8	12	1.22	0.68	
October	88.5	71.5	17.0	86.0	73.2	12.8	79.6				No record			9	2.14	0.70	
November	95.3	72.0	23.5	89.8	75.0	14.8	80.8				73	73.1	69.2	17	6.00	0.92	
December	96.0	74.0	22.0	90.1	76.6	13.5	82.5				No record			15	3.53	0.90	
No. of column	1	2	3	4	5	6	7	8	9	10	11	12	13	14	15	16	17

Solar Radiation and Barometer (columns 8, 9, 10): No instruments for observation.

Prevailing winds (column 17): No observations recorded.

REMARKS:

Instruments used:

1. Thermometer, standard . Murray and Heath.
2.   ,, maximum . Casella A 92 /\
3.   ,, minimum .   ,,   A 102 /\
4.   ,, dry bulb .   ,,   A 743 crown.
5.   ,, wet ,, .   ,,   A 742   ,,
6. Rain Gauge .   ,,   No. 4856.

N.B.—In columns 1, 3, 4, the results are exaggerated during the whole year, owing to faulty position of the maximum and minimum thermometer cage.

ZANZIBAR, EAST AFRICA,
18th January 1879.

JOHN ROBB, M.D., Surgeon,
Civil Surgeon.

$$\frac{A}{1}$$

Results of Meteorological Observations taken at Zanzibar, East Africa.

Latitude 6′ 9′ 40″ S., Longitude 39′ 14′ 20″ E.
Barometer cistern about 25 feet above mean tide-level.
Thermometers " 27 " " "
Rain Gauge " 44 " " "
Solar Max. Therm. " 47 " " "

1875.	Thermometer Maximum	Minimum	Range of month	Mean Maximum	Mean Minimum	Mean Daily range	Mean Daily temperature	Solar Radiation Maximum	Solar Radiation Mean	Barometer Mean: corrected and reduced	Hygrometer Degree of humidity. Saturation = 100	Hygrometer Mean Temperature of evaporation	Hygrometer Mean Temperature of dew point	Rain Number of rainy days, one cent and above	Rain Total fall (inches, cents).	Rain Greatest fall in 24 hours.	Prevailing winds.
January	97.5	73.5	24.0	88.4	76.5	11.9	81.4	No instrument.		No observations recorded.	No observations recorded.			9	3.56	1.83	N.
February	92.0	75.0	17.0	88.8	77.3	11.5	81.7							11	3.89	1.25	N.E. & S.
March	89.5	73.0	16.5	87.6	74.6	13.0	82.6							13	3.79	0.69	S., S.W.
April	88.5	71.5	17.0	85.6	76.7	8.9	81.4				78	77.3	74.2	17	18.75	3.57	S.W.
May	86.0	72.5	13.5	81.7	74.9	8.8	79.8	176.0	165.2		81	76.0	73.3	11	9.40	2.52	S.W.
June	84.5	72.7	11.8	82.4	76.1	6.2	78.9	162.5	156.5	29.997	75	74.6	70.9	6	1.15	0.46	S.W.
July	82.0	71.7	10.3	80.1	74.1	6.0	77.1	155.0	154.7	30.031	79	73.6	70.5	8	4.93	1.95	S.W., light.
August	85.2	72.0	11.2	80.7	73.7	7.0	76.9	155.5	155.2	30.031	75	72.1	68.4	8	1.90	1.15	S. light.
September	85.2	73.5	11.7	82.7	74.8	7.8	78.5	157.0	153.0	29.997	70	74.3	70.2	3	0.32	0.16	Var. calms.
October	86.7	74.0	12.7	83.0	76.0	6.9	79.1	166.0	164.5	29.961	70	75.1	70.6	9	8.05	2.53	S., N.W.
November	86.5	75.0	11.5	84.2	77.7	6.5	81.2	177.5	174.2	29.906	64	77.3	72.1	11	5.50	1.42	Var. calms.
December	87.0	76.5	10.5	84.6	78.9	5.6	82.2	176.0	171.8	29.844	69	78.2	73.6	12	6.95	1.79	Steady light N.
No. of column	1	2	3	4	5	6	7	8	9	10	11	12	13	14	15	16	17

REMARKS.

Instruments used:
1. Thermometer, standard . Murray and Heath.
2. " maximum . Casella A 92
3. " minimum " A 102
4. " dry bulb " A 743 crown.
5. " wet " " A 742 "
6. " solar maximum " No. 16355.
7. Rain Gauge " No. 4856.
8. Barometer, Negretti and Zambra " A 270
Correction at 30 inches = .035.
" of att. thermometer = 1°.0.

N. B.—In columns 1, 3, 4, the results are exaggerated for the first four months of the year, owing to faulty position of the maximum and minimum thermometer cage.

JOHN ROBB, M.D., *Surgeon,*
Civil Surgeon.

ZANZIBAR, EAST AFRICA,
18th January 1879.

A. 2.

Results of Meteorological Observations taken at Zanzibar, East Africa.

Latitude 6° 9′ 40″ S., Longitude 39° 14′ 20″ E.
Barometer cistern about 25 feet above mean tide-level.

Thermometers	,,	27	,,	,,
Rain Gauge	,,	44	,,	,,
Solar Max. Therm.	,,	47	,,	,,

1876.	THERMOMETER							SOLAR RADIATION		BAROMETER	HYGROMETER			RAIN			Prevailing winds.
	Maximum.	Minimum.	Range of month.	Mean Maximum.	Mean Minimum.	Mean Daily range.	Mean Daily temperature.	Maximum.	Mean.	Mean: corrected and reduced.	Degree of humidity, saturation = 100.	Mean Temperature of evaporation.	Mean Temperature of dew point.	Number of rainy days one cent. and above.	Total fall (inches, cents).	Greatest fall in 24 hours.	
January	85.7	76.5	9.2	84.7	79.6	5.0	82.4	173.5	168.3	29.827	70	77.2	73.0	8	3.57	2.08	N.
February	87.5	75.5	12.0	84.9	79.5	5.3	82.7	169.0	166.6	29.827	68	78.7	73.9	6	2.47	1.31	N.
March	88.5	76.2	12.3	84.9	79.1	5.8	82.1	174.0	169.0	29.958	76	78.0	74.6	15	12.72	2.47	N., S.W., S.S.W., S.
April	85.5	74.5	11.0	81.4	77.5	5.0	80.2	179.5	166.6	29.892	87	75.2	73.6	21	13.84	2.13	S.W., S.S.W., S.S.E.
May	84.5	72.5	12.0	80.1	76.0	5.3	79.3	167.0	158.6	29.965	85	74.0	72.1	18	9.46	3.77	S.W., S., S.S.W.
June	82.0	71.5	10.5	74.5	74.5	5.6	77.6	154.0	150.7	30.041	82	71.4	69.9	6	2.02	0.79	S.W., S., S.S.E.
July	82.0	71.7	10.3	73.9	73.7	6.2	76.7	153.0	151.8	30.063	86	70.2	67.4	6	2.20	0.98	S.W., S.S.W., var.
August	82.0	72.0	10.0	80.1	73.8	6.4	77.0	159.0	155.6	30.032	82	70.8	67.4	7	4.47	3.22	S.W., S., Easting
September	82.7	72.5	10.2	80.9	75.8	7.0	77.5	159.0	159.7	30.040	81	72.0	69.4	9	3.33	1.43	S.W., S., var. N.
October	86.7	76.2	13.5	83.0	78.0	7.1	79.7	164.0	162.7	29.973	77	74.5	71.4	2	0.13	0.10	S.E., light var.
November	87.5	74.2	13.3	84.3	78.3	6.2	81.7	172.5	171.0	29.899	84	75.6	73.4	11	7.37	4.63	S., S.E. into N
December	87.2	75.0	12.2	84.8	78.6	6.1	82.5	171.0	170.2	29.897	82	75.7	73.2	14	9.33	2.81	N., N.E.
No. of column	1	2	3	4	5	6	7	8	9	10	11	12	13	14	15	16	17

REMARKS.

Instruments used:

1. Thermometer, standard . Murray and Heath.
2.   ,,   maximum . Casella A 92
3.   ,,   minimum .   ,,   A 102
4.   ,,   dry bulb .   ,,   A 743 crown.
5.   ,,   wet   .   ,,   A 742 crown.
6.   ,,   solar max. . No. 16355
7. Rain Gauge . . . . No. 4856
8. Barometer, Negretti and Zambra A 270
Correction at 30 inches = .025
    ,, of alt. thermometer = 1°·0

No. of column.

ZANZIBAR, EAST AFRICA,
    18th January 1879.

JOHN ROBB, M.D. *Surgeon,*
    Civil Surgeon.

$\frac{A}{3}$.

Results of Meteorological Observations taken at Zanzibar, East Africa.

Latitude 6° 9' 40" S., Longitude 39° 14' 20" E.
Barometer cistern about 25 feet above mean tide-level.
Thermometers   " 27 " " " "
Rain Gauge   " 44 " " " "
Solar Max. Therm.   " 47 " " " "

| 1877. | THERMOMETER | | | | | | | SOLAR RADIATION | | BAROMETER | HYGROMETER | | | RAIN | | | Prevailing winds. |
	Maximum	Minimum	Range of month	Mean Maximum	Mean Minimum	Mean Daily range	Mean Daily temperature	Maximum	Mean	Mean corrected and reduced	Degree of humidity, Saturation = 100.	Mean Temperature of evaporation	Mean Temperature of dew point	Number of rainy days one cent. and above	Total fall (inches, cents).	Greatest fall in 24 hours.	
January	87·7	79·0	8·7	86·2	80·2	6·0	83·0	179·0	172·3	29·875	81	76·6	74·0	4	1·94	1·05	N.E.E.
February	88·5	79·0	9·5	86·3	80·2	5·9	83·9	187·5	173·8	29·875	80	76·2	73·5	4	0·24	0·16	N., N.E.
March	87·7	77·7	10·0	85·8	80·3	5·5	83·7	170·0	166·8	29·853	80	77·5	74·8	13	4·22	1·00	N.W., E., var.
April	87·5	76·2	11·3	84·2	79·1	5·1	82·0	171·0	164·7	29·809	82	75·4	74·0	16	10·61	2·77	S.W., S.
May	86·7	74·7	12·0	83·5	77·4	6·0	80·6	160·0	157·0	29·961	83	74·8	72·4	15	5·01	1·37	S.W., S.
June	84·2	73·0	11·2	82·0	76·3	5·7	79·2	154·5	132·7	30·066	81	72·7	70·1	6	3·07	1·63	{Easting in afternoon.
July	83·2	72·7	10·5	81·6	75·0	6·5	78·3	152·5	130·2	30·047	83	71·8	69·5	10	2·09	0·91	S. to S.E., N.
August	83·5	73·7	9·7	82·2	75·3	6·9	78·9	159·5	135·6	30·046	85	72·1	69·9	9	3·91	1·70	S. to S.E. Easting.
September	85·5	75·0	10·5	83·5	76·5	7·0	80·1	159·7	157·3	29·973	84	73·0	70·7	10	1·73	0·50	S. to S.E., N.
October	86·5	75·0	11·5	84·1	76·9	7·2	80·8	167·0	162·7	29·942	85	73·8	71·8	15	5·93	0·98	S.S.E. to E. to N.
November	85·7	76·0	9·7	83·4	77·9	5·5	81·3	169·5	164·8	29·858	87	75·4	73·5	21	13·11	2·21	{Var. through E. to N.
December	87·0	76·0	11·0	84·9	78·8	6·1	83·0	171·0	166·5	29·855	84	76·9	74·7	16	11·82	4·74	{E., E.S.E., S.S.E. {Var. from 8th, {steady northerly.
No. of column	1	2	3	4	5	6	7	8	9	10	11	12	13	14	15	16	17

REMARKS.

Instruments used:

1. Thermometer, standard . . . Murray and Heath.
    maximum . . . . . Casella A 92
2.   "   minimum . . . . . " A 102
3.   "   dry bulb . . . . . " A 743 crown.
4.   "   wet . . . . . " A 742 "
5.   "   solar maximum . . . No. 19355.
6. Rain Gauge . . . . . " No. 4850.
7. Barometer, Negretti and Zambra . . . A 270
8. Correction at 30 inches =   025.
    " at att. thermometre =   1·0.

JOHN ROBB, M.D. *Surgeon,*
Civil Surgeon.

ZANZIBAR, EAST AFRICA,
18th January 1879.

I

$$\frac{A}{4}$$

Results of Meteorological Observations taken at Zanzibar, East Africa.

Latitude 6° 9' 40" S., Longitude 39° 14' 20" E.
Barometer cistern about 25 feet above mean tide-level.
Thermometers   " 27 "   "   "   "
Rain Gauge   " 44 "   "   "   "
Solar Max. Therm. " 47 "   "   "   "

1878.	THERMOMETER Maximum	Minimum	Range of month	Mean Maximum	Mean Minimum	Mean Daily range	Mean Daily temperature	SOLAR RADIATION Maximum	Mean	BAROMETER Mean, corrected and reduced	HYGROMETER Degree of humidity Saturation=100	Mean Temperature of evaporation	Mean Temperature of dew point	RAIN Number of rainy days one cent and above	Total fall (inches, cents)	Greatest fall in 24 hours	Prevailing winds.	Remarks.
January	88.7	78.7	10.0	86.6	80.1	6.5	84.0	192.0	165.1	29.981	82	77.5	75.0	8	2.26	0.81	N.E. steady till 22nd, S. and a week of calms.	
February	89.0	76.0	13.0	87.0	80.5	6.4	85.1	167.0	164.7	29.869	83	78.1	75.7	11	5.05	1.11	N.E. till 22nd, then southerly and calms.	
March	90.5	77.0	13.5	87.2	80.8	6.4	85.0	170.0	167.8	29.864	83	78.3	76.0	9	2.79	0.69	N. and N.E. until mid-month, variable through into E. into S. and S.W.	Thunder.
April	87.7	76.5	11.2	85.2	79.0	6.1	82.8	167.0	159.5	29.880	81	76.3	73.7	14	15.87	3.58	Southerly in W. and E., very high tide on 18th.	
May	87.5	72.3	15.2	84.3	77.8	6.5	81.8	158.5	159.1	29.958	82.5	75.3	73.0	5	5.97	3.50	W.S.W. through S. into S.S.E., steady southerly.	
June	85.2	72.7	12.5	82.5	75.7	6.8	79.7	160.5	154.0	30.015	82.0	73.2	70.8	7	2.61	0.96	S.W. through S. into S.S.E.	
July	83.7	72.7	11.0	81.8	74.7	7.0	77.8	160.5	149.8	30.007	81	71.2	68.5	4	1.27	0.60	W.W.S. through S. in S.S.E., calms and light, N. at end of month.	
August	84.7	74.5	10.2	82.0	75.4	6.5	78.4	162.0	156.2	30.014	84	72.5	70.3	8	1.51	0.55	W. through S. in E., variable calms, small S.W. on 2 days.	
September	84.5	71.2	13.3	82.0	74.7	7.3	77.9	159.0	154.6	30.019	83	71.2	68.8	9	2.79	0.72	Variable W. into E. through S., 2 days to N. and E., 12 mornings calm.	
October	85.7	73.7	12.0	83.5	75.8	7.7	79.3	166.5	161.7	29.948	83	72.1	69.7	8	2.52	1.07	Variable through S. and E. to N., 16 days to N. variable, 25 mornings calm.	Thunder.
November	87.0	75.5	11.5	84.7	77.9	6.7	81.2	168.0	164.6	29.933	84	74.7	72.5	11	4.95	1.36	19 days N. variable, 5 calm mornings, S.E. to S. through E. variable.	Thunder.
December	86.7	75.7	11.0	84.7	78.7	5.9	82.1	174.0	168.2	29.853	85	75.7	73.6	7	8.70	3.62	Steady N. through N.E. into E., 9 calm mornings, 2 days W. and S.	Thunder.
No. of column	1	2	3	4	5	6	7	8	9	10	11	12	13	14	15	16	17	No. of column.

ZANZIBAR, EAST AFRICA,
18th January 1879.

Instruments used : as in Tables $\frac{A}{2}$ and $\frac{A}{3}$

JOHN ROBB, M.D. Surgeon,
Civil Surgeon.

B.

Monthly Mean Results of Meteorological Observations taken at Zanzibar, East Africa, during the years 1874-78.

Latitude 6° 9' 40" S, Longitude 39° 14' 20" E
Barometer cistern about 25 feet above mean tide-level.
Thermometers   „   27   „   „   „   „
Rain Gauge   „   44   „   „   „   „
Solar Max. Therm. „   47   „   „   „   „

Months	Thermometer		Mean of maximum solar radiation.	Barometer Mean corrected and reduced.	Hygrometer			Rain		General direction of wind.
	Mean daily temperature.	Mean daily range.			Mean degree of humidity, Saturation = 100.	Mean temperature of evaporation.	Mean temperature of dew point.	Mean number of rainy days, one cent and above.	Mean total fall (inches and cents).	
January	82.9	5.8*	168.6*	29.851*	79.·+	77.0†	74.1†	7.·	2.33	N.E., E., calms, S
February	83.1	5.8†	168.0†	29.853*	78.·+	77.4†	74.3†	78	2.99	N.E. E. in afternoon.
March	83.4	5.9*	167.8*	29.858*	80.·+	77.9†	75.2†	12·	5.92	N., N.E., var. W.
April	81.7	5.4*	164.0†	29.873*	83.2	76.6	74.3	16.8	14.84	Southerly in W. and E.
May	80.3	5.9*	157.0†	29.961*	82.·	74.8	72.4	12.·	6.96	W.S.W., S.S.E., S.
June	78.9	6.0*	153.0†	30.029†	80.4	73.1	70.4	5.8	2.09	S.W. into S.S.E. E.
July	77.5	6.4†	151.7†	30.037†	80.6	71.7	69.0	6.4	2.31	W.S.W., S., S.S.E., N. (?)
August	77.7	6.7†	154.1†	30.030†	81.8	71.9	69.3	8.2	2.49	W., S., E., var. calms.
September	78.4	7.2†	158.8†	30.002†	80.8	72.7	69.9	8.6	1.86	W., E., S., calms northing.
October	79.7	7.2†	162.9†	29.956†	78.7†	73.8†	70.8†	8.6	3.75	S., E., N., calms var.
November	81.2	6.2†	168.6†	29.904†	78.4	75.2	72.1	14.2	7.38	S.E., E., N., calms var.
December	82.4	5.9†	169.1†	29.867†	80.·+	76.6†	73.7†	12.8	8.06	N.E., N., steady, calm mornings.

Remarks.

Instruments used.
1. Thermometer, standard . . . Murray and Heath.
2.   „   maximum . . . . Caselia A 92 ⋀
3.   „   minimum . . . .   „   A 102 ⋀
4.   „   dry bulb . . .   „   A 743 crown.
5.   „   wet. „ . .   „   A 742   „
6.   „   solar maximum   „   No. 16355.
7. Rain Gauge . . . .   „   No. 4856.
8. Barometer, Negretti and Zambra . A 270 ⋀
Correction at 30 inches = .025.
       „   of att. thermometer = 1°.0.

N.B.—The averages of three years marked thus *, four „, †.

ZANZIBAR, EAST AFRICA,
18th January 1879.

JOHN ROBB, M.D., *Surgeon,*
Civil Surgeon.

C.

Yearly Results of Meteorological Observations taken at Zanzibar, East Africa, during the years 1874–78.

Latitude 6° 9′ 40″ S., Longitude 39° 14′ 20″ E.
Barometer cistern about 25 feet above mean tide-level.
Thermometers   " 27 " " " " "
Rain Gauge   " 44 " " " " "
Solar Max. Therm.   " 47 " " " " "

YEAR	THERMOMETER							SOLAR RADIATION		BAROMETER	HYGROMETER			RAIN			REMARKS.
				Mean								Mean					
	Maximum of year.	Minimum of year.	Range of year.	Maximum of year.	Minimum of year.	Daily range.	Daily temperature.	Maximum of year.	Mean of year.	Mean: corrected and reduced.	Mean degree of humidity Saturation=100.	Temperature of evaporation.	Temperature of dew point.	Number of rainy days shewing one cent. and above.	Total fall of year (inches, cents.).	Greatest fall in 24 hours.	
1874	96·0	69·0	27·0	86·2	75·0	11·2	80·5	No instruments.			81·4	74·7	72·1	120	46·11	3·74	Instruments used:
1875	97·5	71·5	26·0	84·3	75·9	8·3	80·0	177·5	162·0	29·966	73·6	75·4	71·5	118	68·25	3·57	1. Thermometer, standard . . . Murray and Heath.
1876	88·5	71·5	17·0	82·6	76·6	5·9	79·9	179·5	162·5	29·939	79·5	74·4	71·6	123	70·88	4·63	2. " maximum . . . Casella A 92 ⋀
1877	88·5	72·7	15·8	83·9	77·8	6·1	81·3	187·5	161·9	29·926	82·8	74·7	72·4	129	63·68	4·74	3. " minimum . . . " A 102 ⋀
1878	90·5	71·2	19·3	84·3	77·6	6·7	81·3	174·0	160·2	29·936	82·8	74·6	72·3	101	56·20	3·62	4. " dry bulb . . . " A 743 crown.
Average results	89·1*	71·8*	17·3*	83·6*	77·3*	6·2*	80·6*	179·6*	161·6*	29·944	80·0	74·7	72·3	120·2*	61·02*	4·06*	5. " wet " . . . " A 742 "
No. of column.	1	2	3	4	5	6	7	8	9	10	11	12	13	14	15	16	6. " solar, maximum . . . No. 16355.

7. Rain Gauge . . . No. 4856.
8. Barometer, Negretti and Zambra . . . " A 270 ⋀
   Correction at 30 inches— .02.
   " of att. thermometer— 1·6.

No. of column.

* Average results of three years only (1876–78), because of bad exposure of maximum and minimum thermometer cage during 1874 and portion d 1875.

ZANZIBAR, EAST AFRICA,   JOHN ROBB, M.D., *Surgeon.*
18th January 1879.   *Cecil Surgeon.*

D.

Table shewing the number of days in each month for the years 1875—78 on which were recorded Thunder and Lightning, Lightning only, or Thunder only, at Zanzibar, East Africa.

Latitude 6° 9′ 40″ S., Longitude 39° 14′ 20″ E.

MONTH.	Lightning and Thunder.				Lightning seen, Thunder not heard.				Thunder heard, Lightning not seen.				REMARKS.
	1875.	1876.	1877.	1878.	1875.	1876.	1877.	1878.	1875.	1876.	1877.	1878.	
January	2	5	1	1	2	2	2	3	2	2	1	3	
February	2	3	2	6	2	3	…	…	2	3	3	3	
March	2	8	7	3	2	…	…	…	2	7	8	8	
April	2	1	3	1	…	…	…	4	6	5	2	2	
May	1	…	…	1	…	…	…	…	1	…	…	…	
June	…	…	…	…	…	…	…	…	…	…	…	…	
July	…	…	…	…	…	…	…	…	…	…	…	…	This table has been prepared because it has been written that thunder is very seldom heard at Zanzibar.
August	…	…	…	…	…	…	…	…	…	…	…	…	
September	…	…	…	3	…	…	…	…	…	1	…	…	
October	…	…	1	3	…	…	…	…	…	1	…	…	
November	1	4	2	3	…	…	…	…	3	5	3	3	
December	5	6	5	8	…	1	1	1	3	6	2	3	

JOHN ROBB, M.D. Surgeon,

Civil Surgeon.

ZANZIBAR, EAST AFRICA,

18th January 1879.

K

E.

Chart shewing the Comparative Fluctuations of the Mean Daily Temperature during the Five Years 1874–78.

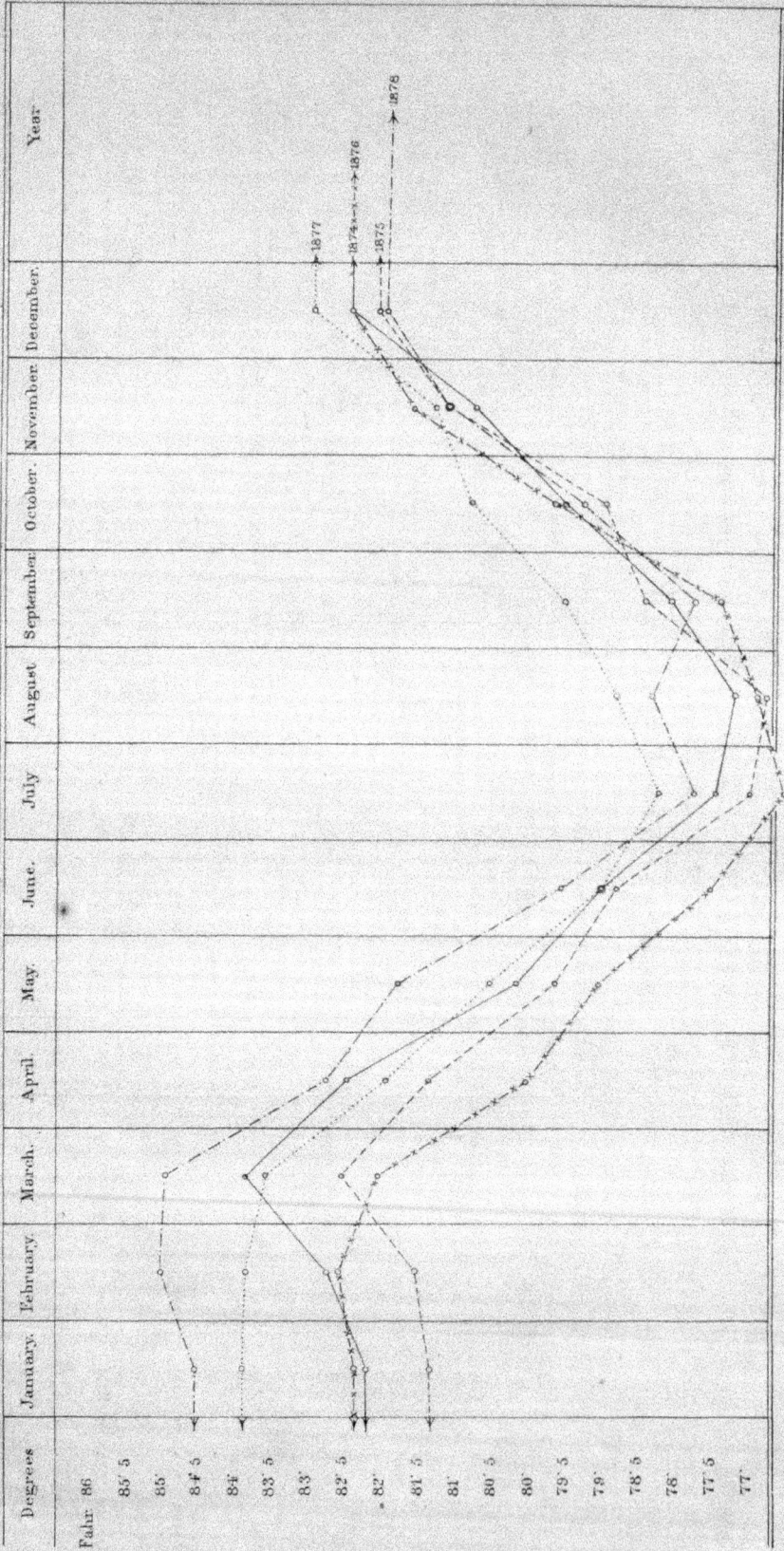

JOHN ROBB, M.D., *Surgeon,*
Civil Surgeon.

ZANZIBAR, EAST AFRICA,
18th January 1879.

Lithographed at the Surveyor General's Office, Calcutta, August 1879.

F.

Chart shewing Comparatively the Mean Monthly Barometric Pressure during the Five Years 1874–78 inclusive.*

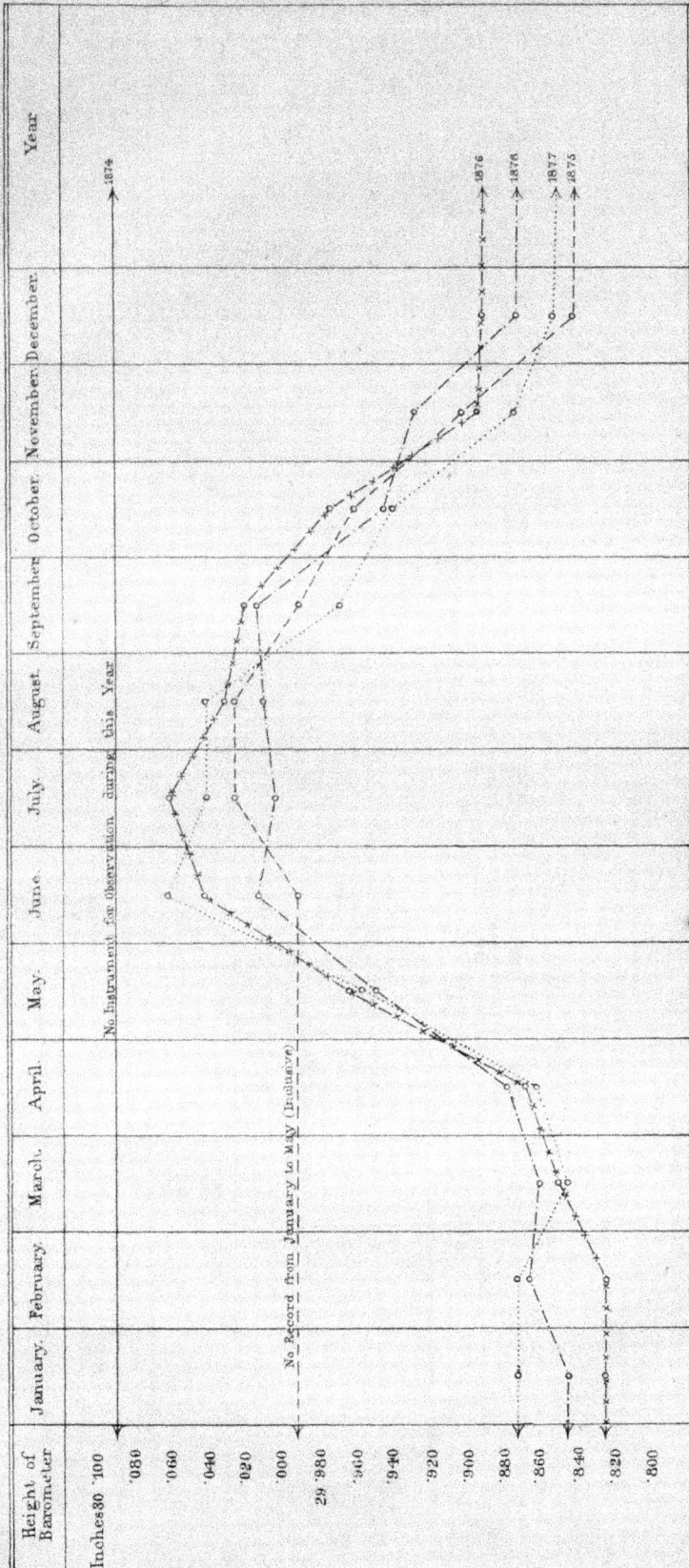

* This ought to have been written " during the period from the middle of 1873 to the end of 1878."

JOHN ROBB, M.D., *Surgeon,*
Civil Surgeon.

ZANZIBAR, EAST AFRICA,
18th January 1879.

Lithographed at the Surgeon General's Office, Calcutta, August 1879.

G.

Chart shewing Comparatively the Degree of Humidity during the years 1874–78 inclusive.

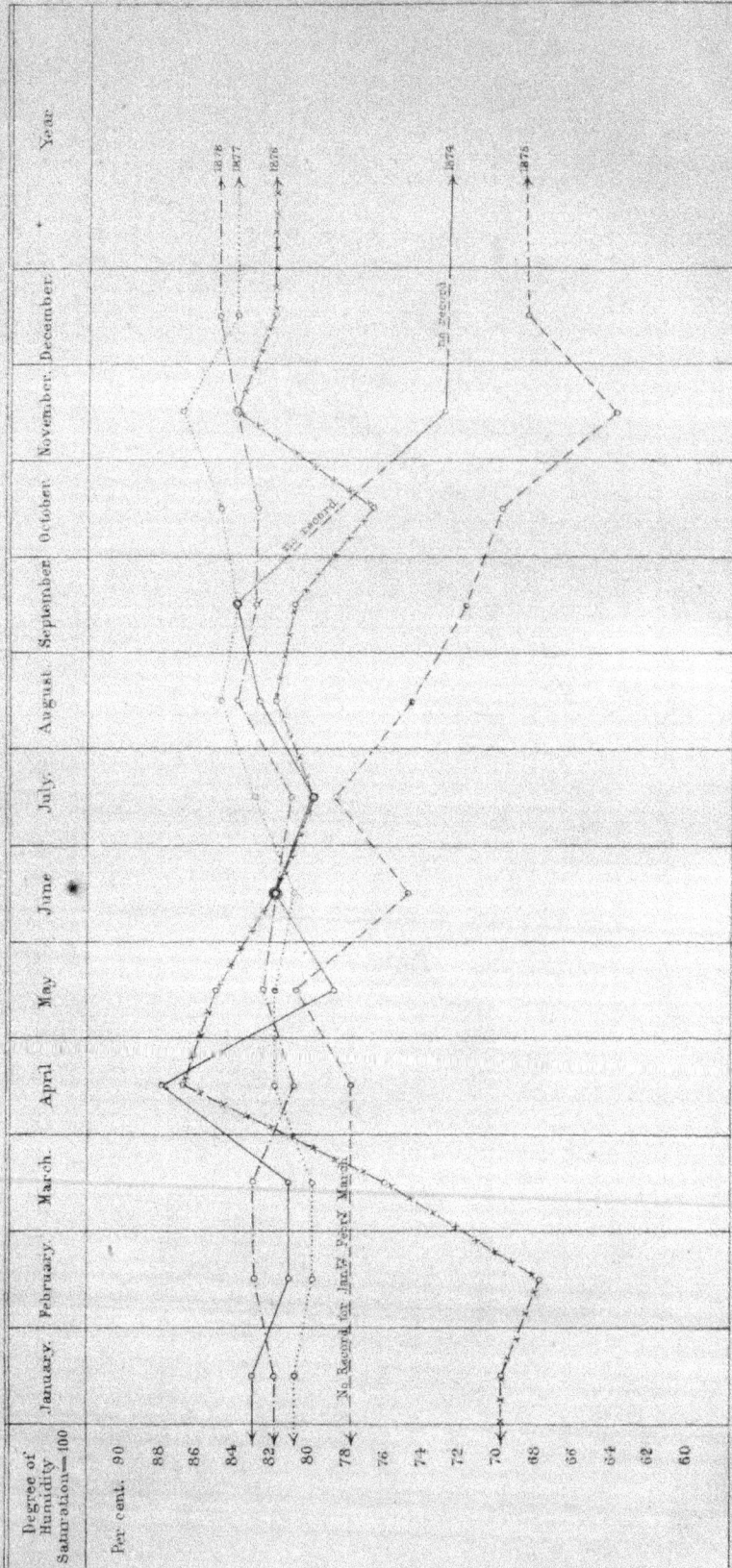

Degree of Humidity Saturation=100	January.	February.	March.	April.	May.	June.	July.	August.	September.	October.	November.	December.	Year

Per cent. 90
88
86
84
82
80
78
76
74
72
70
68
66
64
62
60

No Record for year. Per Month.

1878
1877
1876
1874
1875

ZANZIBAR, EAST AFRICA,
18th January 1879.

JOHN ROBB, M.D., *Surgeon,*
Civil Surgeon.

Lithographed at the Surveyor General's Office, Calcutta, August 1879.

H.

Year 1874, at Zanzibar, East Africa.

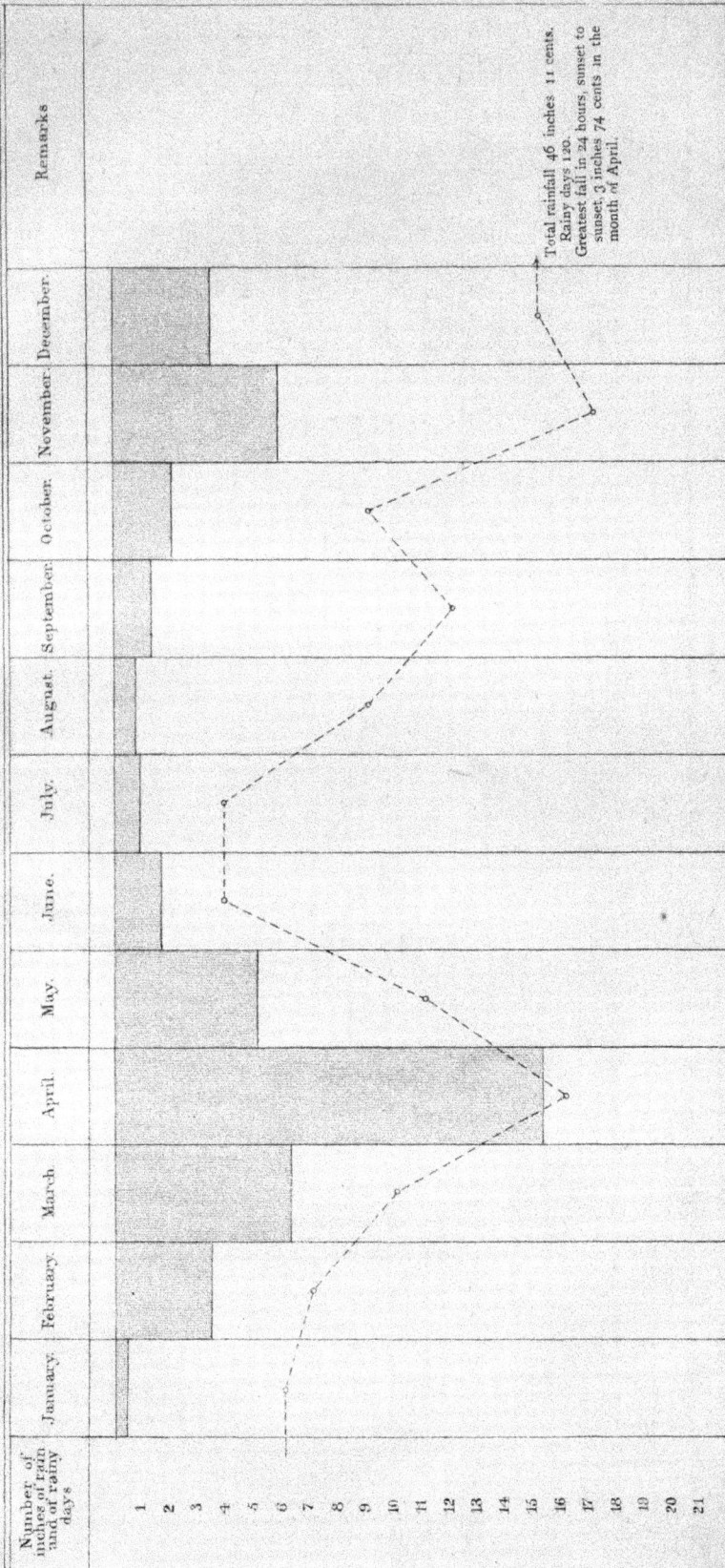

Chart shewing in diagram the Depth of Rain (black tint) and the number of Rainy Days (dotted line) on which one cent (and upwards) was registered.

Number of inches of rain and of rainy days	January.	February.	March.	April.	May.	June.	July.	August.	September.	October.	November.	December.	Remarks

Remarks: Total rainfall 46 inches 11 cents. Rainy days 120. Greatest fall in 24 hours, sunset to sunset, 3 inches 74 cents in the month of April.

ZANZIBAR, EAST AFRICA,
18th January 1879.

JOHN ROBB, M.D., *Surgeon,*
Civil Surgeon.

Lithographed at the Surveyor General's Office, Calcutta, August 1879.

$\dfrac{H}{1}$.

Chart shewing in diagram the Depth of Rain (black tint) and the number of Rainy Days (dotted line) on which one cent (and upwards) was registered.

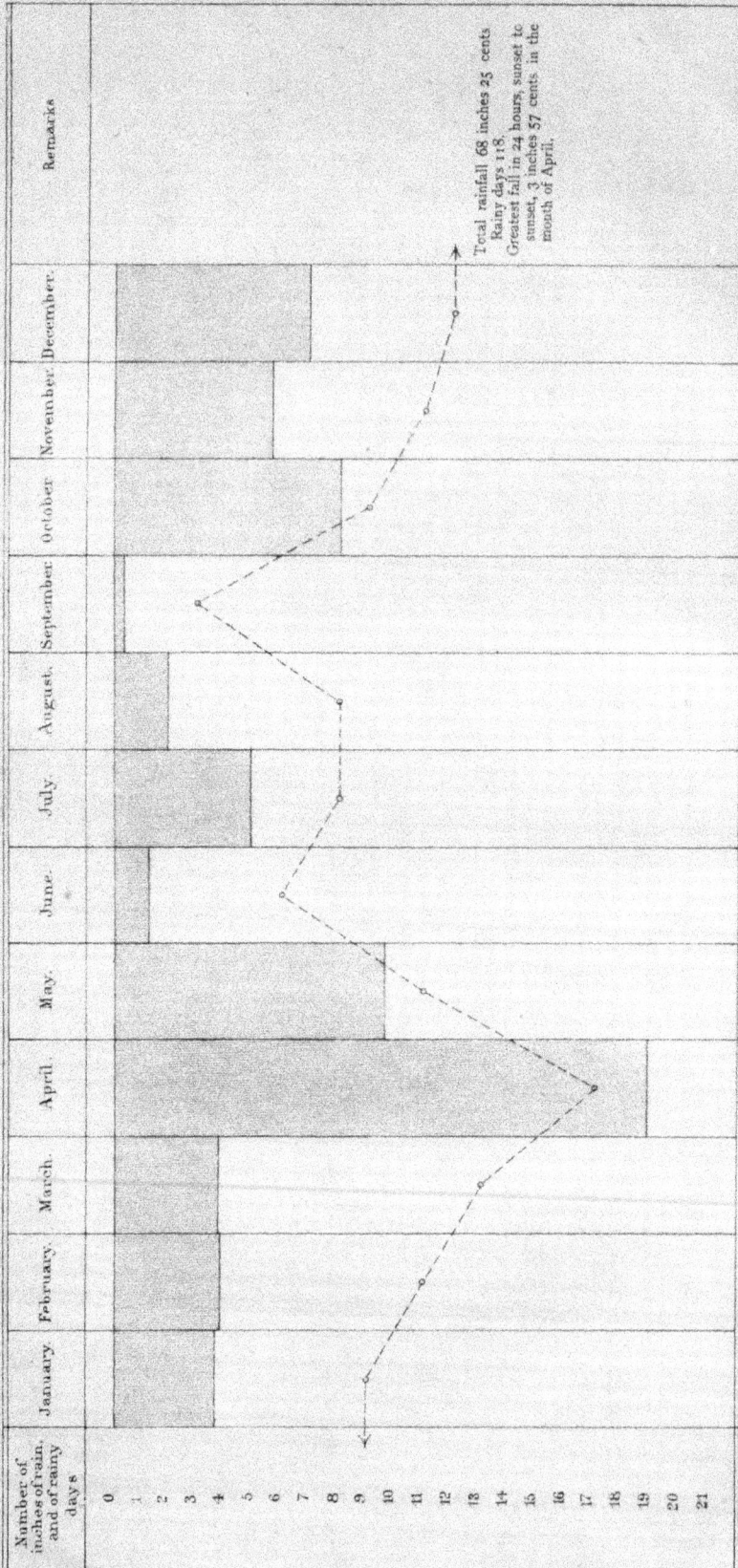

Year 1875, at Zanzibar, East Africa.

Number of inches of rain, and of rainy days	January.	February.	March.	April.	May.	June.	July.	August.	September.	October.	November.	December.	Remarks

Total rainfall 68 inches 25 cents
Rainy days 118.
Greatest fall in 24 hours, sunset to sunset, 3 inches 57 cents in the month of April.

ZANZIBAR, EAST AFRICA,
18th January 1879.

JOHN ROBB, M.D. Surgeon,
Cenl Surgeon.

Lithographed at the Surveyor General's Office, Calcutta, August 1879.

Year 1876, at }
Zanzibar, }
East Africa. }

$\frac{H}{2}$.

Chart shewing in diagram the Depth of Rain (black tint) and the number of Rainy Days (dotted line) on which one cent (and upwards) was registered.

Remarks

Total rainfall 70 inches 88 cents.
Rainy days 123.
Greatest fall in 24 hours, sunset to sunset, was 4 inches 6½ cents in the month of November.

Number of inches of rain, and of rainy days	January.	February.	March.	April.	May.	June.	July.	August.	September.	October.	November.	December.

0
1
2
3
4
5
6
7
8
9
10
11
12
13
14
15
16
17
18
19
20
21

JOHN ROBB, M.D., Surgeon,
Civil Surgeon.

ZANZIBAR, EAST AFRICA,
18th January 1879.

Lithographed at the Surveyor General's Office, Calcutta, August 1879.

Year 1877, at } Zanzibar, East Africa. }

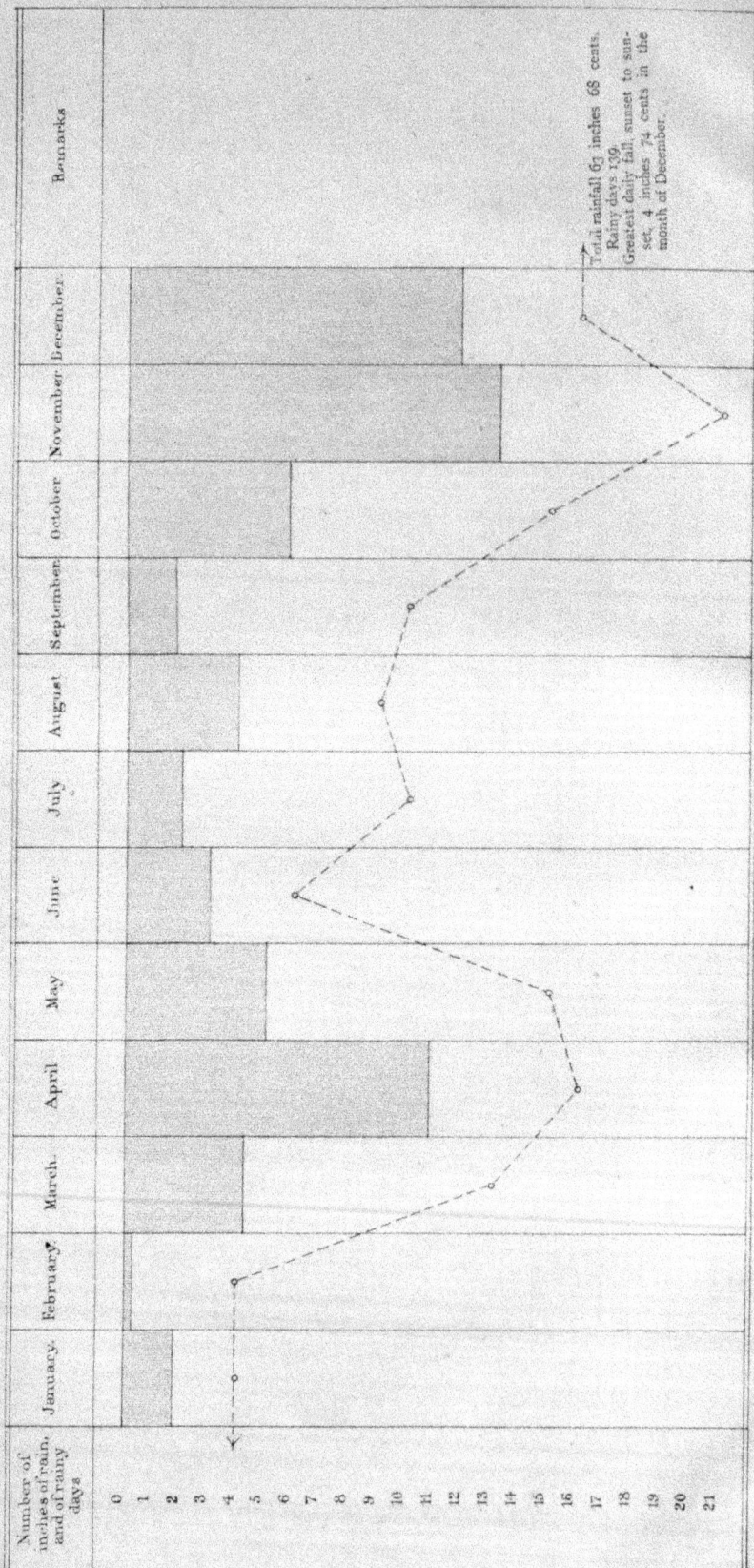

$\dfrac{H}{3}$.

Chart shewing in diagram the Depth of Rain (black tint) and the number of Rainy Days (dotted line) on which one cent (and upwards) was registered.

Number of inches of rain, and of rainy days	January.	February.	March.	April.	May.	June.	July.	August.	September.	October.	November.	December.	Remarks

Total rainfall 67 inches 68 cents. Rainy days 139. Greatest daily fall, sunset to sunset, 4 inches 74 cents in the month of December.

ZANZIBAR, EAST AFRICA,
18th January 1879.

JOHN ROBB, M.D., Surgeon,
Civil Surgeon.

Lithographed at the Surveyor General's Office, Calcutta, August 1879.

$\dfrac{H}{4}$.

Year 1878, at Zanzibar, East Africa. } Chart shewing in diagram the Depth of Rain (black tint) and the number of Rainy Days (dotted line) on which one cent (and upwards) was registered.

Number of inches of rain and of rainy days	January.	February.	March.	April.	May.	June.	July.	August.	September.	October.	November.	December.	Remarks.
0													
1													
2													
3													
4													
5													
6													
7													
8													
9													
10													
11													
12													
13													
14													
15													
16													
17													
18													
19													
20													
21													

Remarks: Total rainfall 56 inches 20 cents. Rainy days 101. Greatest fall in 24 hours, sunset to sunset, 3 inches 62 cents in the month of December.

ZANZIBAR, EAST AFRICA,
18th January 1879.

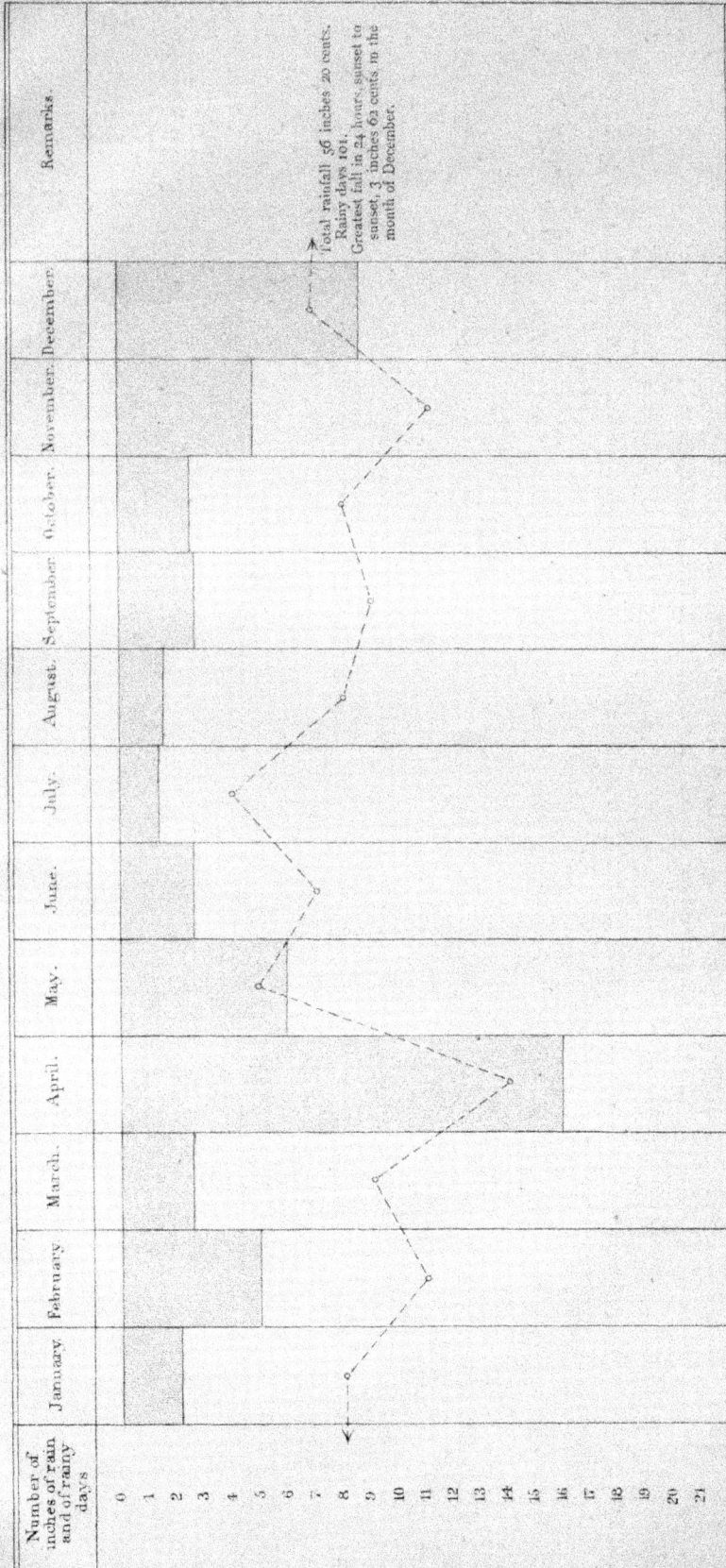

JOHN ROBB, M.D., *Surgeon,*
Civil Surgeon.

Lithographed at the Surveyor General's Office, Calcutta, August 1879.